M000167026

IN GOD'S IMAGE

IN GOD'S IMAGE

An Anthropology of the Spirit

Michael Welker

*The 2019/2020 Gifford Lectures
at the University of Edinburgh*

Translated by Douglas W. Stott

WILLIAM B. EERDMANS PUBLISHING COMPANY
GRAND RAPIDS, MICHIGAN

Published simultaneously in German as *Zu Gottes Bild: Eine Anthropologie des Geistes* by the Evangelische Verlagsanstalt in Leipzig, 2021, and in English by Wm. B. Eerdmans Publishing Co.

This English edition published by
Wm. B. Eerdmans Publishing Co.
4035 Park East Court SE, Grand Rapids, Michigan 49546
www.eerdmans.com

© 2021 Michael Welker
All rights reserved
Published 2021
Printed in the United States of America

27 26 25 24 23 22 21   1 2 3 4 5 6 7

ISBN 978-0-8028-7866-3 (hardcover)
ISBN 978-0-8028-7874-8 (paperback)

Library of Congress Cataloging-in-Publication Data

Names: Welker, Michael, 1947– author. | Stott, Douglas W., translator.
Title: In God's image : an anthropology of the spirit / Michael Welker; translated by Douglas W. Stott.
Other titles: Zu Gottes Bild. English
Description: Grand Rapids, Michigan : William B. Eerdmans Publishing Company, 2021. | "The Edinburgh Gifford Lectures, 2019/2020." | Includes bibliographical references and index. | Summary: "The 2019/2020 Gifford Lectures at the University of Edinburgh, in which Michael Welker explores the concepts of the human spirit and the divine spirit within the bounds of natural theology"—Provided by publisher.
Identifiers: LCCN 2020032274 | ISBN 9780802878663 (hardcover) | ISBN 9780802878748 (paperback)
Subjects: LCSH: Theological anthropology. | Image of God. | Spirit. | Holy Spirit. | Human beings.
Classification: LCC BL256 .W43513 | DDC 218—dc23
LC record available at https://lccn.loc.gov/2020032274

Unless otherwise noted, Scripture quotations are taken from the New Revised Standard Version of the Bible.

Dedicated to Ulrike, Susanne,
and Christiane Welker

CONTENTS

Preface

This book was prompted by my invitation to deliver the Gifford Lectures 2019/2020 in Edinburgh. I am profoundly grateful to my Scottish colleagues for this honor, especially the Gifford Lectureship Committee, Principal Professor Peter Mathieson, and Professors Stewart Jay Brown, David Fergusson, Larry Hurtado†, Mona Siddiqui, Alison Elliot, and Emma Wild-Wood. I am also grateful to Sarah Lane-Ritchie and Joshua Ralston for their reflections and comments in the Gifford Seminar. Let me also thank Mark Newman and his colleagues from the University of Edinburgh administration for their careful preparation and organization of the lecture series, Susan Halcro for a wonderful poster and leaflet templates, and Andrew Johnson for serving as the social media host for the lecture series. I thank the University of Edinburgh and the University of Heidelberg for making the presentation of the lectures accessible on YouTube.

The anthropology presented here attempts to accommodate the guidelines and expectations that the founder of these lectures, Adam Lord Gifford, formulated in his testament in 1885 concerning contributions to natural theology (see in this regard the first lecture).

Above all, it aims at a deeper and more nuanced understanding of the human spirit and the divine Spirit as a sound basis for natural theology and theology in general. In the power of this spirit, humanity can realistically be ennobled by calls to justice, freedom, truth, and peace and thereby transformed into a joyful and loving "image of God." Not only religion but also politics, law, public civil-societal morals, the academy and broader education, the family, the media, and the health-care and medical systems are all capable of incorporating and strengthening this powerful spirit.

At the same time, this anthropology of the spirit questions several concepts, ideas, and theories that have in vain tried to serve the purpose of natural theology, such as an abstract theism with its untenable understanding of divine omnipotence ("God, the all-determining reality"). This anthropology also problematizes theories of "natural law." Not only "has this instrument become blunt," as Joseph Ratzinger stated in a famous conversation with Jürgen Habermas, but from its beginnings in the Corpus Iuris Civilis it has also had to struggle with inner inconsistencies in its attempts, for example, to understand "nature and life" as salvific terms. The sobering truth is that natural life lives indispensably at the cost of other life, and an honest, rigorously consistent "natural law" is inevitably the law of the stronger. This spirit-anthropology also challenges a one-sided intellectualization of the spirit, as fruitful as it has been, and an abstract dualism of spirit and body. It recommends replacing many of the traditional binary and dualistic forms of thought and perceptions that dominated human thinking in the past by cognitive, ethical, and religious sensitivities for creative multimodal spirit-constellations in thought and reality.

This anthropology has been shaped by the profound dejection I experienced in the face of twentieth-century German history, then by subsequent liberating experiences and by the theological and philosophical education I received at German universities and in international and interdisciplinary cooperation over several decades. It has also been shaped by my conviction that a lax attitude or even hostility over against the sustaining support of liberal democracies that promote and protect justice and freedom and in the face of increasing anti-intellectual emotionalization in politics and religion endangers the very groundwork and soul of civil human society. My broad educational background in the German tradition has been enhanced by numerous guest professorships and invited lectures and especially by international and interdisciplinary research projects that have continued over the years in Heidelberg, Chicago, Princeton, Cambridge (UK), and Atlanta.

The lectures published here have profited enormously from a great many discussions and cooperative research opportunities over the past years, especially with my Heidelberg doctoral candidates from fifteen countries and with colleagues from Heidelberg and at numerous universities internationally. Sources of both inspiration and opportunities for learning have included several projects in the Science and Theology Dialogue, in the Law and Religion Dialogue, in interreligious discourse, and in the incipient cooperation between theology and economics. In these contexts, I am especially grateful to John Polkinghorne (Cambridge), John Witte Jr. (Emory), William Schweiker (Chicago), and Jürgen von Hagen (Bonn).

Beyond the circle of my colleagues at the Heidelberg Theological Faculty, I received invaluable stimulation and impetus in recent years from Hans-Jürgen Abromeit, Jan Assmann, Heinrich Bedford-Strohm, Michael Bergunder, Rüdiger Bittner, Armin von Bogdandy, Chun Chul, Sarah Coakley, Celia Deane-Drummond, Markus Dröge, Hans-Joachim Eckstein, Gregor Etzelmüller, Johannes Eurich, Sándor Fazakas, David Fergusson, Elisabeth Schüssler Fiorenza and Francis Fiorenza, Michael Fishbane, Alon Goshen-Gottstein, Berndt Hamm, Tonio Hölscher, Wolfgang Huber, Jörg Hüfner, Larry Hurtado, Bernd and Christine Janowski, Andreas Kemmerling, Kim Jae Jin, Kim Myung Yong, Matthias Konradt, Cornelis van der Kooi, Andreas Kruse, Peter Lampe, Norbert Lohfink, Frank Macchia, Christoph Markschies, Patrick D. Miller, Jürgen Moltmann, Piet Naudé, Friederike Nüssel, Bernd Oberdorfer, Manfred Oeming, Oh Sung-Hyun, Stephen Pickard, Hanna Reichel, Risto Saarinen, Konrad Schmid, Eberhard Schmidt-Assmann, Ingrid Schobert, Andreas Schüle, Helmut Schwier, Christoph Schwöbel, Dirk Smit, Heike Springhart, Jan Stievermann, Philipp Stoellger, Christoph Strohm, Guy Stroumsa, Kathryn Tanner, Klaus Tanner, Gerd Theissen, Günter Thomas, Christiane Tietz, Miroslav Volf, Koos Vorster, Henco van der Westhuizen, Irmgard and Rudolf Weth, Qu Xutong, and Peter Zimmerling.

I am especially grateful to my wife, Ulrike Welker, for our fruitful daily discussions and for her untiring support in the preparation of this book. I would also like to thank my coworkers Hans-Joachim Kenkel, Christine Böckmann, David Reissmann, Daniel Stil, and Viola von Boehn for technical help.

Let me express my deep gratitude to Douglas W. Stott for, yet again, his excellent translation. The spirit of personal and theological friendship that sustains and shapes our work together is constructively shared and enhanced by Barbara Wojhoski and Ulrike Welker.

I am grateful to William B. Eerdmans in Grand Rapids and the Evangelische Verlagsanstalt in Leipzig for their essentially concurrent publication of these lectures.

I am dedicating this book to the three people from whom I have learned more in the field of anthropology than from all the learned treatises and books I have read over the years.

—M. W.
Heidelberg, May 2020

Lecture 1

THE BREADTH AND ABYSSES
OF HUMAN EXISTENCE

According to the will of the founder, Adam Lord Gifford, the Gifford lectures are "to promote, advance, teach and diffuse the study of natural theology." That is, they are to serve "true knowledge of God" and advance knowledge of "the relations that human beings bear to God" and "knowledge of the nature and foundation of ethics or morals, and of all obligations and duties thence arising." Moreover, as implied by the term "natural theology," a strictly scientific approach is demanded, "without reference to or reliance upon any special exceptional or so-called miraculous revelation." Of course, at this point Christian theologians must leave aside for a moment the central tenet of faith—namely, that God is revealed to human beings in Jesus Christ.[1] And finally, these lectures are

1. Excellent anthropologies based on a theology of revelation include David Kelsey, *Eccentric Existence: A Theological Anthropology*, 2 vols. (Louisville: Westminster John Knox, 2009); Gerhard Sauter, *Das verborgene Leben: Eine theologische Anthropologie* (Gütersloh: Gütersloher Verlag, 2011). Wolfhart Pannenberg combines perspectives from both the theology of revelation and natural theology in his essential *Anthropology in Theological Perspective* (Edinburgh: T&T Clark, 1985; Philadelphia: Westminster, 1985); and his *Systematic Theology*, vol. 2 (Grand Rapids: Eerdmans, 1994), 175–324. Cf. the

1

to address a "general and popular audience," including people critical of or indifferent to religion.

I perceive two fundamental ways of meeting these challenges. One is to start with scientific and related historical research and then try to reach out to human "belief" and "faith" in their various forms, without, however, losing touch with empirical reality. Agustín Fuentes's Gifford Lectures of 2018, "Why We Believe: Evolution, Making Meaning, and the Development of Human Nature,"[2] are an excellent example of the approach that takes us from scientifically accessible nature and history to the realms of religion and theology.

The other approach, the one I intend to pursue, begins with cultural and social realities and incorporates into that discussion part of the wealth of philosophical, cultural, religious, and theological impulses. Throughout, however, it is ever alert to secure, within the framework of the program of "natural theology," the connection with empirical and historical research and investigation as well as with commonsense perception. I describe this approach as "realistic theology." Thirty years of dialogue with natural scientists has considerably enhanced my awareness of the rich possibilities of such a theological research and interdisciplinary cooperation.

I view Lord Gifford's will and guidelines as a challenge whose relevance remains undiminished here at the beginning of the twenty-first century. The concern of many distinguished thinkers in the past to investigate to what

---

critique of Pannenberg's anthropology in Thomas Pröpper's *Theologische Anthropologie*, 2 vols. (Freiburg: Herder, 2011), 414–36.

2. Agustín Fuentes, "Why We Believe: Evolution, Making Meaning, and the Development of Human Nature," https://www.gifford lectures.org/lecturers/agust%C3%ADn-fuentes.

extent the central content of religion and theology can genuinely be made accessible to *all* people is by no means an antiquated one. Immanuel Kant's grand program of comprehending "religion within the limits of reason alone"[3] remains vibrant even today, at least as a topic of discussion. And the burning desire to strengthen interreligious and interdisciplinary communication and shared searches for truth and conditions of peace underscore the vibrancy of such a project.[4]

The overall theme of these lectures is "In God's Image: An Anthropology of the Spirit." The fundamental question is whether and, if so, how human beings in their natural, social, and cultural existence can be understood as the image of God (*imago Dei*). Oddly, perhaps, this first lecture must necessarily question the very assumption that human beings are indeed made in the image of God. For it illuminates not only the tension between human weakness and wretchedness, on the one hand, and the enormous power and grand destiny of human beings as such, on the other, but also the alarming susceptibility of human beings to seduction; their violent, aggressive, destructive tendencies; and their outright maliciousness. Emphasizing the breathtaking breadth of human existence through simple

3. Immanuel Kant, *Religion within the Boundaries of Mere Reason*, trans. Allen Wood (Cambridge: Cambridge University Press, 1998).

4. Perspectives from natural theology can also come to bear in interdisciplinary research concerning the notion of "implicit religion" in secular societies and in commitments to interreligious understanding. See, e.g., Günter Thomas, *Implizite Religion: Theoriegeschichtliche und theoretische Untersuchungen zum Problem ihrer Identifikation* (Würzburg: Ergon, 2001); Michael Welker and William Schweiker, eds., *Images of the Divine and Cultural Orientations: Jewish, Christian, and Islamic Voices* (Leipzig: EVA, 2015); Alon Goshen-Gottstein, ed., *Friendship across Religions: Theological Perspectives on Interreligious Friendship* (Eugene, OR: Wipf & Stock, 2018).

reference to "human weakness" and the "grand destiny" of human beings, however, by no means excuses us from drawing equal attention to the dreadful and repugnant abysses of that same existence.

Negative aspects of the impressive breadth of human existence also include the dull, apathetic complacency toward the human race's massive self-endangerment and toward the immense scale on which hatred and violence are being sown today. We are especially oppressed by the unthinking or simply lethargic attitude toward socially brutal behavior on many levels. Here one might mention especially the ecological brutality that ranges from overt destruction, to the denial and cover-up of dangerous developments, to dull indifference, even on a global scale. Indeed, do not these abysses of human existence render any talk of human beings as the "image of God" absolutely preposterous? Worse yet, with what sort of God are we then dealing if human beings, even in their abysses, are to be conceived as the "image of God"? Given these considerations, and taking our natural-theological point of departure from human beings themselves, is Lord Gifford's program of articulating a scientifically sound, universally comprehensible, and ethically edifying understanding of God not doomed to failure from the very outset?

Immanuel Kant concludes his *Critique of Practical Reason* with the poignant remark, "Two things fill the mind with ever new and increasing admiration and awe, the oftener and the more steadily we reflect on them: *the starry heavens above and the moral law within*." The starry heavens above, Kant goes on to say, with their "countless multitude of worlds," annihilate, "as it were, my importance as an *animal creature*, which after it has been for a short time provided with vital power, one knows not how, must again give back the matter of which it was formed to the planet it inhabits (a mere speck in the universe)." By contrast, the second ground of admiration and awe for Kant "infinitely elevates my worth as an *intelligence* by my personality, in which the moral law reveals to me a life independent of animality and even of the whole sensible world."[5]

The biblical Psalter is even more drastic than Kant in its description of the breadth of human existence between frailty and sublimity, finitude and grand destiny. On the one hand, human beings are but "dust . . . their days are like grass; they flourish like a flower of the field; for the wind passes over it, and it is gone, and its place knows it no more" (Ps. 103:14–16). Yet human beings are nonetheless made only "a little lower than God" and have been "crowned . . . with glory and honor" (Ps. 8:5).

Although the following lectures address these statements from a variety of angles, let us put them aside for a moment, change perspective, and focus instead on the "general and popular audience." Rather than following Lord Gifford's suggestion that one view that audience as those to whom we might impart knowledge, however, let us instead query them, here at the beginning of the twenty-first century, concerning how they themselves already understand the breadth of human existence. Probably not a single person would think to mention, as does Kant, the tension between the almost inevitable annihilation of one's own significance and reality, on the one hand, and one's elevation through the moral law, on the other. Just as little would we expect anyone to mention the tension between mortals being "mere dust" and yet simultaneously only "a

5. Immanuel Kant, *Critique of Practical Reason and Other Works on the Theory of Ethics*, trans. Thomas Kingsmill Abbott, 5th rev. ed. (London: Longmans, Green, 1898), 260, translation altered.

little lower than God." So how *does* popular culture understand the breadth of human existence today?

Human Charisma and Radiant Power, and the Dangers of Emotionalized Public Sentiment

One area in popular culture where the tension and breadth of human existence are clearly discernible is elite athletic competition, which is followed all over the world through the media. The enormous resonance elicited by competitive sports has deep anthropological roots. These sports focus intensely on that unique area of physical human existence that through an extreme engagement of body and mind produces extraordinary performances with global visibility. Physically and mentally gifted elite athletes transform into a superior performance what in and of itself is, to take but one example, the simple act of moving forward, an act most people are also capable of performing. The media make it possible for millions of spectators to become emotionally and passionately engaged in and identify with such performances. The fascinating anthropological power elicited by these sports heroes derives simply from their being simultaneously close to us and yet in possession of enormous charisma and radiant personal presence.

No one ever ran the 100 meter and 200 meter events as fast as Usain Bolt—and yet I, too, understand what it feels like to run as if one's life depended on it. No one plays soccer today as well as Lionel Messi—and yet I, too, am quite able to kick a soccer ball around and be inspired by its flight.

The radiant force of attraction of such successful athletes, however, is based not only on a given performance but also on spectators' admiration for their astonishing capacity for both physical *and* mental training, endurance, and persistence. For as a rule, years of training inevitably also involve years of self-discipline and asceticism.

The intense emotional attachment of spectators to elite athletes whose performances attain Olympic heights or who play on winning teams is always accompanied by equally intense feelings of community; and it is not just the media that heartily welcome such resonance but also political leaders. Victorious teams, moreover, also generate enthusiasm through successful *team play*. Such play, precisely for the sake of the team as a whole, results from individual team members engaging in unconditional self-assertion, on the one hand, and creative self-withdrawal, on the other. Perfect cooperation is rewarded, and the players' own joy is transmitted to their fans.

Elite athletic performance, however, also reveals the enormous mood changes such athletes experience between individual triumph in victory and individual despair in defeat. Such mood swings also reflect the ambivalence experienced by spectators through their own intensive, emotionally charged, and shared identification with these athletes. We all have witnessed such ambivalence following national and international competitions in the more popular sports. Who can resist being swept up in the exuberant joy unleashed following a victorious team performance of top athletes? But failure, too—a lost match, a missed chance—generates experiences of mass shock and pain that in the heat of the moment are by no means assuaged by the fact that such pain generally passes rather quickly and indeed just as quickly transforms into optimistic hope for future victory.

We witness this familiar phenomenon of emotionally charged sentiment, however, not merely in elite sports but also in actions and demonstrations of civil societies when they usefully and creatively sound the alarm in oppressive situations. Under the dominance of organized politics, however, this phenomenon can easily acquire precarious forms whenever marches, parades, and mass rallies are functionalized to manipulate people politically or even to discipline them. Initially people may merely be voluntarily demonstrating loyalty, rejoicing with others in various communal places or stadiums. They demonstratively express that they belong to a particular circle of people who are engaging on behalf of a specific cause. All too easily, however, they can lose sight of a specific cause and become "hangers-on" who self-righteously demonstrate with those who "call the good good and the bad bad" (Niklas Luhmann).

Such emotionally charged sentiment, however, quickly derails when politicized moral aggression and hatred are intentionally roused, stoked, exploited, and sustained. It is enormously alarming to see how politics and propaganda today are successively compromising the free media, legal systems, and scientific and scholarly research in what were formerly free nations. For these same manipulated emotions can easily become utterly unfettered, expressing themselves then in racist, aggressively chauvinistic, or bellicose sentiment and strife. Although such belligerent disputes may initially generate feelings of triumphant enthusiasm among the masses, sooner or later they generally lead to universal misery and suffering.[6]

Ideologies and wars that incite hatred and aggression can prompt people to commit horrible crimes against the very idea of humaneness, and as such against humanity.

---

6. See Konrad H. Jarausch, *Broken Lives: How Ordinary Germans Experienced the Twentieth Century* (Princeton: Princeton University Press, 2018).

The bureaucratically organized mass murder of millions of people in German concentrations camps during the Nazi period still vividly attests the most profound abyss of horror. The mass sexual enslavement of two hundred thousand Korean and Chinese women as "comfort women" by the Japanese during the Second World War provides an enduring image of human atrocity. Such violent excesses can as a rule be stopped only by colossal processes of destruction, as illustrated by so many cities of Germany—all in ruins—after the war. It was in the extreme form of the atomic bomb that the twentieth century vividly illustrated the unnerving possibilities of global destruction through man-made weapons.

Paths into Danger, Misery, and Ruin (Hannah Arendt)

Hardly anyone has presented a more penetrating examination of the political and moral paths that lead populations and nations into danger, misery, and ruin than has Hannah Arendt, who wrote from a perspective of profound existential experience as a threatened German Jew forced to live as a stateless person in the United States for several years. Her work deftly weaves this personal experience into her unique historical, political, and sociological training in the phenomenon of mass psychology and her equally profound and penetrating conceptual talent. In 1948 she published the volume *Six Essays* with a dedication to her Heidelberg teacher and doctoral advisor, Karl Jaspers. In it she expresses her gratitude to this "Dear Most Honored One" from whom she learned not only how to "find [her] way around in reality without selling [her] soul to it" but also that "the only thing of importance is not philosophies but the truth, that one has to live and think in the open and not in one's own little shell, no matter how comfortably furnished it is, and that necessity in whatever form is only a will-o'-the-wisp that tries to lure us into playing a role instead of attempting to be a human being."[7]

Despite such appreciation, she nonetheless cannot help remarking, "It is consequently almost impossible for us Jews today not to ask any German we happen to meet: What did you do in the twelve years from 1933 to 1945? And behind that question lie two unavoidable feelings: a harrowing uneasiness at placing on another human being the inhuman demand to justify his existence and the lurking suspicion that one is face to face with someone who worked in a death factory or who, when he learned something about the monstrous crimes of the government, responded with: You can't make an omelet without breaking eggs."[8]

In his preface to the German edition of Arendt's monumental work *The Origins of Totalitarianism*,[9] Karl Jaspers acknowledges the "spirit of truthfulness" in her work and her service to "human dignity" (13). Arendt's work, he says, "seeks through knowledge to contribute to the moral-political thinking that makes human self-assertion possible amid the rootless chaos of our time" (12).

Arendt focuses on the most extreme forms of tyranny by exhaustively examining the history and emergence of the reigns of terror in German National Socialism and in Stalinism. Total rule and total power pay no attention to

7. Hannah Arendt, *Essays in Understanding, 1930–1954*, ed. Jerome Kohn, trans. Robert Kimber and Rita Kimber (New York: Harcourt Brace Jovanovich, 1994), 212–14.

8. Arendt, *Essays in Understanding*, 214.

9. Hannah Arendt, *The Origins of Totalitarianism*, 2nd ed. (New York: Harcourt Brace Jovanovich, 1958). English pagination appears in parentheses in the following discussion.

the positive rule of law. Instead, they organize instruments of terror whose goal is to systematically eradicate and eliminate any and all opposition. Arendt illuminates the brutal destruction not only of "freedom as a living political reality" but also—though difficult to conceive—of "the lawless, fenceless wilderness of fear and suspicion which tyranny leaves behind" (466).

Terror organizes the masses such that "it is as though their plurality had disappeared into One Man of gigantic dimensions" (465–66). "One's familiar orientation in the world is replaced by a compulsion to allow oneself to be swept along by the torrent of preternatural, natural, or historical forces."[10] Masses ruled by terror, moreover, eventually also surrender even their own sense for self-preservation.

In almost all her writings, Arendt concentrates on determining how even in preliminary or nascent forms of political violence one might discern and possibly even thwart this human susceptibility to total domination and terror. She penetratingly asks about the specific powers that might be engaged against these "devastating sandstorms" or against this "deluge" (478). Her brilliant treatises thus focus on discerning in an exemplary fashion not only sequences of dramatic political repression but also those processes of creeping social degeneration that have often proved remarkably inefficient in substituting "stability for chaos, honesty for corruption, authority and trust in government for decay and disintegration."[11]

10. From the German edition: *Elemente und Ursprünge totaler Herrschaft: Antisemitismus, Imperialismus, totale Herrschaft*, 20th ed. (Munich: Piper, 2017), 966.

11. Hannah Arendt, "The Freedom to Be Free," in Hannah Arendt, *Thinking without a Banister: Essays in Understanding*, vol. 11, ed. Jerome Kohn (New York: Schocken Books, 2018), 369.

Arendt describes paths that lead to endangerment and catastrophe, paths along which people are essentially trained to be dull, unfeeling, witless, and crude. She discerns the oppressive indifference with which during the postwar period Germans wandered about among the desolate ruins of their country. After being confronted herself with the abysses of the Nazi dictatorship as an observer at the Eichmann trial in Jerusalem, she provocatively challenged world opinion with her description of the "banality of evil." In the introduction to her 1973 Gifford Lectures in Aberdeen,[12] she remarks:

> I was struck by a manifest shallowness in the doer that made it impossible to trace the uncontestable evil of his deeds to any deeper level of roots or motives. The deeds were monstrous, but the doer—at least the very effective one now on trial—was quite ordinary, commonplace, and neither demonic nor monstrous. . . . The only notable characteristic one could detect in his past behavior as well as in his behavior during the trial and throughout the pre-trial police examination was something entirely negative: it was not stupidity but *thoughtlessness*. . . . His cliché-ridden language produced on the stand . . . a kind of macabre comedy.[13]

Discerning in this perpetrator a complete renunciation of any thinking connection with reality, she wonders, "Might the problem of good and evil, our faculty for telling right from wrong, be connected with our faculty of

---

12. Hannah Arendt, *The Life of the Mind*, vol. 1, *Thinking*; vol. 2, *Willing*; 2 vols. in 1 (New York: Harcourt Brace Jovanovich, 1978), 1:4.
13. Arendt, *Life of the Mind*, 1:4.

thought?"[14] She sought an answer to this question in her Gifford Lectures with their obvious orientation to Kant's three critiques—namely, "Thinking," "Willing," and an unfinished addendum on "Judging."

What she finds is that this epidemic, ethically disastrous thoughtlessness is by no means restricted merely to political disasters associated with totalitarian rule and its consequences. She sees with prophetic clarity that the mass spread of egoism can just as easily unhinge or grind into gray conformity even those allegedly free civil associations that constitute part of late-modern pluralistic consumer societies. Her considerable skepticism concerning the vitality of politically and morally pluralistic democracies raises the disturbing specter for her that their publics and social groups, too, and with them the potential for freedom, are vulnerable to being fatally undermined. She apparently does not trust the capacity of late-modern societies to generate ever anew those particular civil associations capable of politically shaping the potentials of freedom in the public sphere amid the constant flux of dissonance and concerted action. She fears that the sphere of public politics, overwhelmed by egoistic and distracted privatism, will eventually become stultified.[15]

Arendt's diagnoses of such dramatic, creeping political disintegration consciously distinguish between "power" and "violence" or between "power" and "domination." Max Weber had defined "power" as the possibility of imposing one's own will on the behavior of others: "'Power' is the probability that one actor within a social relationship will

14. Arendt, *Life of the Mind*, 1:5.
15. See Hannah Arendt, *The Human Condition*, 2nd ed. (Chicago: University of Chicago Press, 1998), esp. 38–40; Michael Welker, *Kirche im Pluralismus*, 2nd ed. (Gütersloh: Kaiser Verlag, 2000), 18–24.

be in a position to carry out his own will despite resistance."[16] Arendt understands Weber's concept of power as "violence," as "domination" that tends toward repression. By contrast, she elevates "power" as the human capacity for coming to an agreement and uniting through unforced communication for the sake of cooperative action. "Power corresponds to the human ability not just to act but to act in concert."[17]

In his astute essay "Hannah Arendt's Concept of Power" (1976),[18] Jürgen Habermas initially concurs that the "basic phenomenon is not the instrumentalizing of another's will for one's own purposes but the formation of a common will in a communication aimed at agreement."[19] Habermas acknowledges in several publications Hannah Arendt's extraordinary political sensitivity. As early as 1992, he asserts that "Hannah Arendt's diagnosis—that stateless persons, refugees, and those deprived of rights would come to symbolize this century—has proved frighteningly accurate. The 'displaced persons' that the Second World War left in a devastated Europe have long since been replaced by asylum seekers and immigrants flooding into a peaceful and prosperous Europe from the South and the East. The old refugee camps can no longer accommodate the flood of new immigrants."[20]

16. Max Weber, *Economy and Society: An Outline of Interpretive Sociology*, ed. Guenther Roth and Claus Wittich (Berkeley: University of California Press, 1978), 53.

17. Hannah Arendt, *On Violence* (New York: Houghton Mifflin Harcourt, 1970), 44.

18. Jürgen Habermas, *Philosophical-Political Profiles* (Cambridge, MA: MIT Press, 1983), 171–88.

19. Habermas, *Profiles*, 172.

20. Jürgen Habermas, *Between Facts and Norms: Contributions to a Discourse Theory of Law and Democracy* (Cambridge, MA: MIT Press, 1996), 507–8.

At the same time, as a political realist, he laments the limitations of Arendt's political theory, maintaining that she became the victim of an antiquated understanding of politics no longer applicable to modern circumstances[21] when she harshly condemned the economic and administrative integration of politics and similarly excluded from politics the necessity of a strategic engagement of power: "The concept of the political must also extend to the strategic competition for political power and to the application of that power within the political system itself."[22] That is to say, the strategic exercise of power is politically indispensable. Criticizing it as a manifestation of violence and excluding it inevitably leads to a loss of contact with political reality.

Realistic Visions of Liberation and Freedom?

Hannah Arendt's diagnoses concerning the emergence of rule based on violence and terror and of the concurrent processes of humanitarian disintegration, coarsening, and suffering among broad portions of a population are both extremely astute and extremely instructive. But does the same assessment hold true for her visions of constructive, salutary alternatives and countermovements? Her suggestions are doubtless quite moving, as is, for example, her image of a poor rural population that is brought into a big city for the first time and is now assured that, indeed, this is your possession. But does not such imagery reflect an element of social romanticism that sooner heightens feelings of helplessness over against perilous political and moral developments?

21. Habermas, *Profiles*, 239.
22. Habermas, *Profiles*, 245.

Although Arendt acknowledges the difficulty in conceiving how a community based on freedom and peace might actually be structured, she nonetheless confronts her critics and doubters with various critical reservations and constructive suggestions. And she repeatedly engages in criticism. Philosophers, she maintains, have paid too little attention to human beings in their plurality; "political freedom is possible only in the sphere of human plurality, and on the premise that this sphere is not simply an extension of the dual I-and-myself to a plural We."[23] She intensifies this reproach by criticizing the insufficient bipolar thinking used in ethics and in social diagnostics—and not merely in a general sense and in connection with what might be called "healthy human understanding," but also among philosophers and sociologists. Indeed, many distinguished thinkers have employed this conceptual framework of person-to-person relations (for instance, "Aristotle's friend; Jaspers' beloved; Buber's thou").[24] Arendt objects that such bipolar understanding, even in the form of "the 'inner action' in which I 'appeal' to myself or to the 'other self,'" is neither a "guarantee of truth" nor "paradigmatic for the political sphere."[25]

23. Arendt, *Life of the Mind*, 2:200.

24. Arendt, *Life of the Mind*, 2:200. Freud's ego and super-ego and their derivatives in more recent psychological and philosophical theories might also be mentioned here. Cf. Judith Butler's critique of "subject" constructions and "binary oppositions" in numerous more recent studies, esp. those inspired by Freud (Judith Butler, *Bodies That Matter: On the Discursive Limits of "Sex"* [London: Routledge Classics, 2011]; Judith Butler, "My Life, Your Life: Equality and the Philosophy of Non-Violence," 2018 Gifford Lectures, Glasgow, https://www.giffordlectures.org/lecturers/judith-butler-0).

25. Arendt, *Life of the Mind*, 2:200.

Although person-to-person relationships are important in the daily life of individuals, they cannot grasp complex social circumstances. Nor does a hypothetical multiplicity of such bipolar relations yield any realistic concept of actual social constellations. Such also applies to the idealizing notions of deliberative democracies in which all the people are to transform societal circumstances through reasoned dialogue (Habermas and others). Arendt's alternative is "natality"[26] as the source of freedom—that is, insofar as every newborn person has the capacity to make a new beginning. The possibility of saving the world allegedly resides nowhere else but in the capacity for humankind to shape itself continually anew. She also discerns in social developments this power of renewal in the "magic of birth." "And obviously, this mysterious human gift, the ability to start something new, is connected to the fact that every one of us came into the world as a newcomer through birth. In other words, we can begin something because we are beginnings and hence beginners."[27]

Arendt tries to support this view by adducing various anthropological, religious, and political examples, such as Augustine's obscure remark from *De civitate Dei* in which, to counter the erroneous notion of the eternal cycle of souls, he insists that we must start from "some beginning; and this beginning never before existed. That this beginning, therefore, might be, the first man was created."[28] She also repeatedly quotes the well-known phrase from Virgil's fourth Eclogue, "Afresh the mighty line of years begins

26. Arendt, "Freedom to Be Free," 383.

27. Arendt, "Freedom to Be Free," 383.

28. Augustine, *The Works of Aurelius Augustine*, ed. Marcus Dods, vol. 1, *The City of God* (Edinburgh: T&T Clark, 1871), 513.

anew," which became the motto on the reverse side of the great seal of the United States: *Novus ordo seclorum.*

But how is one to react today to such visions of hope in the face of the horrendous fact that in our world 149 million malnourished children under five years of age still suffer from stunted development, and that 49.5 million children under five years of age can be described as "wasted"?[29] According to UNESCO, 617 million children and young people can neither read nor count. According to recent statistics from the International Labour Organization, 152 million girls and boys are forced to work as child laborers—that is, under conditions that rob them of essentially all fundamental rights and opportunities.[30] UNICEF estimates that three to four million children and young people worldwide are forced into child prostitution—not counting the high number of unreported cases. About 250,000 child soldiers were deployed in 2017 in at least nineteen countries (Terre des Hommes International Federation).[31] And worldwide we are shocked by investigations into the countless cases of child abuse by a patriarchal, gerontocratic, and celibate organization of clerics.

Yet another reason for skepticism toward the optimistic paean of natality is that the birth rates of five of the ten

29. Cf. UNICEF, "World Hunger Is Still Not Going Down after Three Years and Obesity Is Still Growing—UN Report," https://www.unicef.org/press-releases/world-hunger-still-not-going-down-after-three-years-and-obesity-still-growing-un.

30. Cf. UNICEF, "Kinderarbeit Weltweit," https://www.unicef.de/informieren/aktuelles/blog/kinderarbeit-fragen-und-antworten/166982.

31. "Kindersoldaten," https://www.tdh.de/was-wir-tun/themen-a-z/kindersoldaten/?gclid=CjoKCQjwuZDtBRDvARIsAPXFx3CUJfOyDkhHxq-uGvdftS9e6EkVS9fUMjzL_vn37KOzcr6Mbxfd-xEaAuuuEALw_wcB.

strongest export nations fall at the bottom end of all the nations of the earth. On the one hand, a blessing of high birth rates quickly becomes a curse without sufficient and stable economic and educational possibilities. On the other hand, initiatives for promoting families and child welfare especially in the economically more stable areas of the world require strong intellectual and institutional impulses. A natural theology or ideology of natality will not be sufficient.

Hannah Arendt herself draws attention to this lack of urgently needed intellectual impulses in volume 2, *Willing*, of her posthumously published Gifford Lectures, *The Life of the Mind*. Here she reflects self-critically on the limitations of a mentalistic, bipolar understanding of the mind and the spirit. She describes the frightening isolation of the thinking self and also the misery of a merely solipsistic freedom of the will.[32] That is to say, here, too, both thinking and willing seem to break down as powers of resistance. The question is thus whether there is any way out of this desolate situation.

32. "Just as thinking prepares the self for the role of spectator, willing fashions it into an 'enduring I' that directs all particular acts of volition. It creates the self's *character* and therefore was sometimes understood as . . . the source of the person's specific identity. Yet it is precisely this individuation brought about by the Will that breeds new and serious trouble for the notion of freedom. . . . Nothing indeed can be more frightening than the notion of solipsistic freedom—the 'feeling' that my standing apart, isolated from everyone else, is due to free will, that nothing and nobody can be held responsible for it but me myself. The will with its projects for the future challenges the belief in necessity, the acquiescence in the arrangement of the world which it calls complacency." Arendt, *Life of the Mind*, 2:195.

Lecture 2

HUMAN SPIRIT AND DIVINE SPIRIT

This lecture will first unfold a natural theology of the divine Spirit by means of a contemporary example. What one finds is that a purely intellectual, rational understanding of this Spirit or vague notions that it is a numinous entity that eludes our understanding cannot adequately grasp this Spirit and its workings.

In the second part, I demonstrate how the divine Spirit and the human spirit are multimodal powers that cannot be reduced to entities characterized predominantly by bipolar relations.

Observations on early-childhood mental development in the third part show that the human mind is considerably broader and more complex than the intellectual, rational spirit. Aesthetic and moral powers in coordination with the human body and its natural and social environments must be included to get a full picture of the human spirit.

In the final part, I broaden the perspective on social, political, and religious questions connected to the spirit by turning to a mastermind of the spirit, the philosopher Hegel. Even in his early years, he was interested in a natural theology of the human spirit and of the divine Spirit. In a multimodal fashion, he developed a theological and moral concept of these spirits that ultimately focuses on freedom and justice. Later his philosophy turned to a metaphysical and totalitarian notion of the spirit that, however, cannot but compromise the spirit of freedom.

A Contemporary Natural Theology of the Divine Spirit (John Paul II)

In October 1978, Karol Wojtyła from Poland was elected pope. Eight months later, in June 1979—during the second of his over one hundred trips abroad—he visited his homeland and on June 6 celebrated his first mass there on Victory Square in Warsaw. He concluded with a prayer that electrified his fellow Poles: "And I cry—I who am a son of the land of Poland and who am also Pope John Paul II—I cry from all the depths of this millennium, I cry on the vigil of Pentecost: Let your Spirit descend! Let your Spirit descend and renew the face of the earth, the face of this land! Amen."[1]

Everyone in Poland understood what he said—except perhaps the Communist government, which allegedly wondered whom, exactly, he had summoned. The CIA? A year later, in 1980, strikes erupted in the country, leading to the founding of the labor union Solidarity and—despite numerous violent setbacks—to enduring social, political, and freedom-based transformations in Poland and else-

1. "Homily of His Holiness John Paul II, Victory Square, Warsaw, 2 June 1979," https://w2.vatican.va/content/john-paul-ii/en/hom ilies/1979/documents/hf_jp-ii_hom_19790602_polonia-varsavia .html. Cf. Michael Welker, "Holy Spirit and Human Freedom: A John Paul II Memorial Lecture," *International Journal of Orthodox Theology* 8, no. 1 (2017): 9–30; Polish: Michael Welker, "Duch święty i ludzka wolność," *John Paul II Memorial Lectures* (Warsaw: Centrum Myśli Jana Pawła II / Konrad Adenauer Stiftung, 2018), 181–96.

where.[2] Two decades later, during his eighth, penultimate journey to Poland, John Paul II spoke once more at the site of his legendary 1979 address:[3] "Is not all that happened at that time in Europe and the world, beginning with our own homeland, God's response? Before our eyes, changes of political, social and economic systems have taken place, enabling individuals and nations to see anew the splendor of their own dignity. Truth and justice are recovering their proper value, becoming a challenge for all those who are able to appreciate the gift of freedom."[4]

Justice, truth, and freedom as mentioned in this speech—along with peace and love—are themes that consistently stir the hearts of people in many cultures. They are also central themes in the Bible. Indeed, Paul and other biblical authors explicitly associate these concepts with the activity of the Holy Spirit.[5] In the Old Testament, the classical biblical witness to the "outpouring" of the divine Spirit is the prophet Joel in Joel 3:1–5, and in the New Testament Acts 2:1–13. It is highly noteworthy that biblical accounts of the outpouring of the Spirit explicitly include women and even maidservants (slaves) and young people—that is, not merely the men, who traditionally had the last word in such communities. The New Testament

2. Michał Łuczewski, *Solidarity: Step by Step* (Warsaw: Centre for Thought of John Paul II, 2015); Tomasz Zukowski, ed., *Values of Poles and the Heritage of John Paul II: A Social Research Study* (Warsaw: Centre for Thought of John Paul II, 2009).

3. In Warsaw on June 13, 1999; the square had in the meantime been renamed Piłsudski Square.

4. "Homily of His Holiness John Paul II, Warsaw, Sunday, 13 June 1999," https://w2.vatican.va/content/john-paul-ii/en/homilies/1999/documents/hf_jp-ii_hom_19990613_beatification.html.

5. See, e.g., Rom. 8:10 (justice); 2 Cor. 3:17 (freedom); 2 Thess. 2:13 and John passim (truth); and Rom. 14:17 and Gal. 5:22 (peace).

account in Acts, moreover, also mentions the salutary effects that the outpouring of the Spirit had on numerous other nations, races, and languages. The pope does not address the highly charged and even revolutionary consequences that these biblical witnesses have for the status and treatment of women and against the subordination of young people in patriarchal and gerontocratic communities—not to speak of chauvinistic, xenophobic, and racist environments.

But for a moment let us concentrate on the notion itself of the outpouring of the Spirit. This phenomenon implies that the divine Spirit can be "invoked"—that is, petitioned to descend upon human beings—but also that those receiving this outpouring are in their own turn "summoned" to respond in a life-changing way. The outpouring of the Spirit is a realistic event that within the context of natural theology can be conveyed particularly by way of its effects on human circumstances. For John Paul II also spoke about social, political, economic, and moral transformations with tangible changes for individual persons, an entire nation, and even international relations. And to describe the weave of virtues and values he discerned being mediated by the Spirit, he turned to the grand concepts of truth, justice, freedom, and human dignity.

He considered this development to be "God's response" to the petitionary "invocation" associated with a liturgical event. At the same time, he was clearly aware that these social and political developments were also the fruits of his summons to the people of Poland and to many other supportive powers throughout the world—something many of his addresses during his journeys to Poland underscore. This summons, however, is intimately associated with an invocation of the Spirit. Or more precisely, these remarkable developments were in fact brought about by the countless committed engagements that followed upon the invocation and summons. How might we understand more clearly the cooperative actions of the divine Spirit and the human spirit in this light?

Note: the Status Q. [handwritten marginal note]

The Spirit—a Multimodal and Multipolar Power

The expression "multimodal" has been in common usage only since the twentieth century, particularly since the digital revolution, and primarily in connection with linguistics, media studies, psychology, philosophy, and economics. In business communication, multimodality can, for example, enhance customer satisfaction by providing several contact possibilities between customers and the business, such as text messaging, chats, and social media. Media are multimodal if, for example, they deliver information not just by way of a single medium such as a text but through other media as well, such as speech and images that not only specify a message more clearly but also actually shape it.

By contrast, one speaks of "multipolar" constellations whenever a given constellation (of people, social entities, or even an arrangement of nerve cells) possesses several centers or several poles. The idea of a multipolar world order, for example, envisions a political arrangement with several power centers, enabling the world to be stabilized (or destabilized) by different states or power blocs.[6]

But why in this present inquiry concerning the human spirit and the divine Spirit and their cooperative activities might we profit from a multimodal and multipolar ap-

---

6. I am grateful to Andreas Kemmerling for the discussions of these two terms.

proach? The advantage of understanding the spirit by way of such an approach is that it offers wholly new insights over against dominant forms of the traditional understanding of the spirit. To wit, previous perspectives on the spirit and its effects were distorted by, among other things, attempts to come to an understanding by way of culturally tenaciously rooted bipolar thinking.[7] Notions of the spirit and its effects tended to be reduced to simple relationships (e.g., between God and person; between one human being and another; between the various facets of my interior intellectual, moral, and religious dialogue; and between the act of thinking and what is thought). In situations in which one sensed that the spirit was somehow "more" than could be articulated by bipolar reductions, the remedy in many religious and even secular communities was simply to view it as a mysterious, nebulous, incomprehensible, numinous power. One shifts, as it were, from unequivocal bipolarity over to diffuse plurality and assumes that the divine Spirit is a numinous, transcendent power that descends upon creatures from the beyond like wind and rain. The image of the outpouring of the Spirit "from above"—conceived in a less than rigorous manner—and various biblical statements seemed to support such vague notions. A reflection on John Paul II's invocation and summoning of the Spirit in Warsaw in 1979, however, provides us with a considerably different perspective.

Although the pope was convinced that God did indeed respond to the invocation, that response did not come

7. Cf. Michael Welker, *God the Spirit* (Philadelphia: Fortress, 1994; repr. Eugene, OR: Wipf & Stock, 2013), 279–302; Michael Welker, "The Spirit in Philosophical, Theological, and Interdisciplinary Perspectives," in *The Work of the Spirit: Pneumatology and Pentecostalism*, ed. Michael Welker (Grand Rapids: Eerdmans, 2006), 221–32.

about in some ghostlike, indeterminate fashion. Instead, many people were concretely, profoundly moved and inspired to think, communicate, and act anew and indeed in new ways. In the historical case under consideration here, a considerable role was played by a distinct consciousness not only of divine power but also of open support by the head of the Roman Catholic Church. A key factor in all situations involving the outpouring of the Spirit, however—both past and present—is that the resulting interplay between people does *not* simply remain diffuse and aimless. What emerges is a focused movement. A great many individuals act together, doubtless sometimes even in conflict with one another, and yet always in "re-action" to one another, and it is together, collectively, that their actions bring about grand results. Plural developments of this sort, developments that cannot be traced back to simple cause-and-effect chains, are described as "emergent." As a rule, emergent developments initiated by the outpouring of the Spirit cannot be guided or stopped by simple intervention and are permeated by a healthy measure of free decisions and actions and thus sometimes take surprising turns.

It is extremely important to keep in mind that these developments always focus on specific content, for the divine Spirit does not impart this or that arbitrary impulse. Although even influential thinkers such as Hans Küng or Charles Taylor have repeatedly asserted that people need "some kind of religiously or morally imparted orientation,"[8] this view ignores the important notion of a dis-

---

8. Charles Taylor, *Sources of the Self: The Making of the Modern Identity* (Cambridge: Cambridge University Press, 1989), 28; note also his erroneous assumption that orientations in the moral sphere unfold similarly to those in the natural sphere (48). Hans Küng, *Global Responsibility: In Search of a New World Ethic* (Chestnut Ridge: Crossroad, 1991); and see my review, "Hans Küngs 'Projekt

cernment of spirits. After all, there are not only freedom-oriented spirits but also evil, destructive, and subversive spirits. Think of an evil spirit that spreads hate in a country. The view that a spirit and its effects are from the outset exclusively good is as naive and foolish as the view that morality and religion are always and in all their manifestations charitable and good. Here the differentiation between the divine Spirit, which is always conducive to life, and other spirits, whose effects can be good or evil, is essential.

Recently, and not least under the impression of global ecological self-endangerment, we have heard the assertion that the divine Spirit must be understood as the "spirit of life."[9] And indeed, historically the terms "nature" and "life" have frequently been used with salvific connotations. Unfortunately, a great many illusory concepts associated with "spirit" and "life" also came into circulation as a result of this understanding. For if the spirit brings about "life" in what is essentially an unqualified manner, then it also promotes the growth of tumor cells or the sudden emergence and development of a reign of terror.

Because "nature" and "life" are ambivalent concepts, they are ill-suited for understanding the divine Spirit. After all, all natural, earthly life—without exception—lives indispensably at the cost of other life, thus the formulation of Alfred North Whitehead: "Life is robbery."[10] Precisely

Weltethos': Gutgemeint—aber ein Fehlschlag," *Evangelische Kommentare* 26 (1993): 354–56.

9. Jürgen Moltmann, *The Spirit of Life: A Universal Affirmation* (Minneapolis: Fortress, 1992). Moltmann wants to discover the spirit "in nature, in plants, in animals and in the eco-systems of the earth" (10), to bring together the experience of God and the experience of life, to experience God in all things (34–36), and to theologically qualify vitalism (85–87).

10. Alfred North Whitehead, *Process and Reality: An Essay in Cos-*

this insight prompted the apostle Paul to emphasize the dualism between the flesh and the spirit. The fleshly, bio-logical existence of human beings is unavoidably predatory and frequently sustained by illusions. For it not only lives at the cost of other life but also believes itself capable of doing so for an indefinite period of time through fleshly ac-tivities such as eating and propagation. Paul's radical crit-icism of fleshly existence has frequently offended people, who accuse him of promoting views hostile to the body, to sexuality, and to homosexuality. Such objections fail to see, however, that Paul is in fact making an extremely impor-tant distinction—namely, between flesh and body. For the human body is characterized not only by transitory, pred-atory flesh but also by psyche (soul) and spirit. Indeed, the body is a fascinating entity precisely because of the multiplicity of its constituent parts, their interplay, their mutual sensitivity, and their multifarious radiation. It can both be viewed as the "temple of the Holy Spirit" (1 Cor. 6:19) and adduced as an orienting image for the existence of free spiritual communities.[11]

The petitioning of the divine Spirit and the summons to

mology, Gifford Lectures 1927–28, corrected ed. (New York: Free Press, 1978), 105: "Thus, all societies require interplay with their en-vironment; and in the case of living societies this interplay takes the form of robbery. The living society may, or may not, be a higher type of organism than the food which it disintegrates. But whether or no it be for the general good, life is robbery. It is at this point that with life morals become acute. The robber requires justification."

11. See Michael Welker, ed., *The Depth of the Human Person: A Multidisciplinary Approach* (Grand Rapids: Eerdmans, 2014). See also in that volume Michael Welker, "Introduction," 1–12; Michael Welker, "Flesh—Body—Heart—Soul—Spirit: Paul's Anthropology as an Interdisciplinary Bridge-Theory," 45–57; Gerd Theissen, "*Sarx, Soma*, and the Transformative *Pneuma*: Personal Identity Endan-gered and Regained in Pauline Anthropology," 166–85.

allow oneself to be seized and filled by this Spirit are thus not counting on "nature" as such or on indistinct powers of "life." They focus rather on life's qualified creative powers. John Paul II, undoubtedly inspired by Paul, spoke about the powers of justice, freedom, and truth, as well as about human dignity. Indeed, this emphasis on universal human dignity erects as it were a kind of protective sphere around each and every human being, and in so doing precludes any view of individual human life—for example, in the face of massive global overpopulation—as being superfluous and harmful in and of itself. Vehement debates today about the international obligation to accept refugees or rescue them from distress at sea vividly illustrate the highly charged nature of this topic.

People overcome and seized by the Spirit constitute, on the one hand, multimodal networks and, on the other, multipolar but fluid collectives that need balance and equalization. That is, these are not homogeneous communities "in lockstep." And indeed they instead tend to view fixed hierarchies skeptically, especially when the latter resist attempts by these communities to control or reshape them. Such associations tend to develop both political and legal forms of a division of power. What, then, are the realistic powers of the human spirit to which we genuinely have recourse within this weave of opportunities and crises? Let us begin this investigation with an assessment of the individual human mind and spirit.

An Assessment of Early-Childhood Multimodal Mental Development

Western culture has long valued especially the intellectual faculties of the human spirit. The spirit has been under-

stood primarily as the individual faculty of human thinking. In his splendid work *Sources of the Self: The Making of
the Modern Identity*, Charles Taylor has—beyond this intellectual spirit—illuminated the much richer multimodal
powers of the mental spirit under the titles "Inwardness"
and "The Affirmation of Ordinary Life."[12] He tries to understand the "self in moral space" and the role that the
"voice of nature" plays in the development of self and of
"modern identity."[13]

He emphasizes the importance of critically engaging
with ideologies that place too much trust in the powers of
the sciences or in the orienting powers of group morals.
How can the human spirit develop optimally and avoid
going astray?

A grand philosophical tradition stands behind the intel-
lectualist understanding of the human spirit that conceives
of the spirit first and foremost as thinking—ranging from
the intellectual processing of sense perceptions to the activities of reason. A key text can be found in Aristotle's
Metaphysics, book 12, where he describes how the intellectual activity of reason focuses on, grasps, and thinks about
objects. In this very activity, however, reasoning thought,
precisely by taking up objects into itself, is also thinking
itself. That is, thinking takes as its object not only external
objects and its surroundings but also itself engaged in its
own dynamic activity.

Here thinking moves within a process of completion
and intensification, and this activity of thinking is accompanied by both a sensibility and a striving (emphatic or
not) for precisely such completion. That is, the subtler

12. Taylor, *Sources of the Self*, 111–207, 211–302.
13. Taylor, *Sources of the Self*, 25–107, along with the concluding
evaluation, 305–90.

and richer perception of objects and surroundings moves thinking toward a completion of its conceptual powers, and the enhanced powers in their own turn deepen and expand its broader disclosure of the world. Aristotle refers to the highest intensification—that is, to the perfection of this process—as "divine" and ascribes it to the highest being.[14]

In early-childhood development, we find a vivid illustration of the power of the nascent intellectual spirit and, beyond it, the wealth of the aesthetic and moral mind that accompanies the new life that Hannah Arendt celebrated with the term "natality." A small child points for the first time to a nearby place or object and accompanies the gesture with a sound. Parents are naturally delighted at the first communication of their child in contact with its surroundings and world. After incessant repetitions of this action, they eventually tire of the sound that means "Look! Look! Look!"[15] They decide instead to use the opportunity

14. Cf. Aristotle, *The Works of Aristotle*, vol. 8, *Metaphysica*, trans. W. D. Ross (Oxford: Clarendon, 1928), 1072b; Welker, *God the Spirit*, 283–85.

15. Michael Tomasello, Malinda Carpenter, and Ulf Liszkowski, "A New Look at Infant Pointing," *Child Development* 78 (2007): 705–22; Holger Diessel, "Deixis and Demonstratives," in *An International Handbook of Natural Language Meaning*, vol. 3, ed. Claudia Maienborn, Klaus von Heusinger, and Paul Portner (Berlin: de Gruyter, 2012), 2407–31; http://www.personal.uni-jena.de/~x4diho/Deixis%20and%20demonstratives.pdf, 1–25: "There is a long tradition in western philosophy to define human cognition by formal operations over abstract symbols. . . . However, recent work in cognitive psychology, philosophy, and linguistics has argued that this approach is not appropriate to characterize human cognition. Specifically, it has been claimed that cognitive processes are 'embodied,' i.e., grounded in our bodily experience with the environment. . . . In this view, the sensory and motor activities of the body are important determinants of human cognition, which in turn influences the

for a bit of teaching. "That's a ball!" Joy and delight erupt anew when the child does indeed seize on this new information. And again, once "Ball! Ball! Ball!" becomes fatiguing, the teaching begins anew. "The ball is round!" "The ball is red!"—and again great delight when one beholds language acquisition taking place before one's very eyes. The ascent to the cognitive and linguistic completion of the spirit and to an expanded disclosure of the world can now begin in earnest.

The human spirit, however, is intrinsically richer and more complex than what is usually conceived as a bipolar or at best triadic completion of thought in the form of interplay between object-relation and self-relation (the primitive form of which is simply subject—object—subject-object relationship). We can observe this complexity in what otherwise seem to be the simplest deictic operations in early childhood. What is happening here?

Immediate surroundings are being disclosed. What, for example, has roused the child's interest? What natural or cultural spaces and objects are coming into focus? Even at

---

structure and use of language. . . . There is perhaps no other linguistic phenomenon that is so fundamentally rooted in our bodily experience than deixis" (2). "The frequent combination of demonstratives and deictic pointing is especially striking in early child language. . . . When children begin to produce their first words, at around the age of 15 months, they typically use content words referring to persons, objects, and other entities in their environment; but in addition to these words demonstratives are always among the first and most frequent expressions in early child language. The early appearance of demonstratives is motivated by their communicative function to establish joint attention and their relationship to deictic pointing. The earliest pointing gestures children produce appear a few months prior to the onset of language and can be seen as a sign of the child's emerging ability to engage in triadic interactions, providing a prerequisite for the development of communication and language" (11).

this elementary level, the spirit engages in powerful aesthetic and intellectual operations. For the child, this concentrated perception, this selection from the profusion of optical impressions, is only one of many operations it must carry out and relate. This optical selection and concentration are joined by differentiated, partial control of the body in the form of a raised, outstretched arm and a movement of the hand with the outstretched index finger.

Optical, acoustic, tactile-motor, and imaginative operations must all be coordinated. Under certain circumstances, the child abstracts from the sense of smell—already developed earlier—and from the sense of taste. It is astonishing to consider the complexity of the multimodal network and differentiation that must take place within the child's over-stimulated body before the enormous operation of abstraction and psychosomatic synthesis can emerge in the form of an allegedly "primitive" deictic operation.

Over the course of what Michael Tomasello calls the "nine-month revolution,"[16] the internal complexity of multimodal sensuous reactions in the body is complemented by similarly multimodal communications. Unfortunately, Tomasello speaks in a reductionist fashion of a revolutionary transition from bipolar to triadic constellations, involving a further partner in the relations to the objects of the environment. In fact, the relations are much more complex. The utterance "Look!" accompanying the

16. Michael Tomasello, *The Cultural Origins of Human Cognition* (Cambridge, MA: Harvard University Press, 2001); Stefanie Höhl, "Frühkindliches Lernen in sozialen Interaktionen. Welche Rolle spielt Verkörperung?," in *Verkörperung: Eine neue interdisziplinäre Anthropologie*, ed. Gregor Etzelmüller, Thomas Fuchs, Christian Tewes (Berlin: de Gruyter, 2017), 33–55. See also the more general approach by Shaun Gallagher, *How the Body Shapes the Mind* (Oxford: Clarendon, 2006).

gesture of pointing can draw attention to various primary interests—for example, to the child's affirmed object discovery, to the elicitation of attention from others, and to what some scholars call the child's "imperative" anticipation of connecting response, such as praise, reward, or the object itself being given to the child.

At this level, the multimodal weave of physical perception is being joined by the formation of a rudimentary social milieu. "In this sense, pointing, engaged on the basis of cooperative willingness and social intent, introduces interactions characterized by divided attention focus."[17] It is this divided attention focus that first makes language learning possible. It is also the basis for rudimentary moral communication.

Moral communication, too, seems to commence quite straightforwardly. Parents approve and laugh when the child behaves one way and speak harshly or even remain silent when it behaves differently or inappropriately. At the level of linguistic communication, signals are given such as, "Your mother will be so happy if you do this!" or "Grandfather will be so sad if you don't do that!" The child's sense of its current status is conditioned within a network in which attention is either granted or withheld, or promises

---

17. Nicole Weidinger, *Gestik und ihre Funktion im Spracherwerb bei Kindern unter drei Jahren*, Wissenschaftliche Texte (Munich: Deutsches Jugendinstitut, 2011), 9–10. See also Michael Tomasello, *Origins of Human Communication* (Cambridge, MA: MIT Press, 2008); Jana M. Iverson and Susan Goldin-Meadow, "Gesture Paves the Way for Language Development," *Psychological Science* 16 (2005): 367–71; "In sum, our findings underscore the tight link between gesture and speech, even in children at the earliest stages of language learning. At minimum, gesture is a harbinger of change in the child's developing language system, as it is in other cognitive systems later in development. . . . Gesture may even pave the way for future developments in language" (370).

or threats of such are issued. Rudimentary moral communication is accompanied by a variety of either deliberate or emergent educational processes.

Thus in order to grasp the multimodal power of the spirit with respect to the organization of human faculties, we must add *communicative processes connected to deixis* to the weave of thinking, willing, and complex aesthetic perception of one's surroundings. Only then do we get an idea of its overwhelming capacities even at the most basic embodied mental level.

The primary relational point and framework, however, consistently remain one's individual, concrete physical existence, guided, on the one hand, by a multimodal sensuous network and, on the other, by socially interactive and linguistically mediated processes of communication and the radiance of natural and cultural surroundings.

This mental spectrum of activity is also accompanied by a multifarious interest or drive toward completion. The disclosure of self and the world through the operations of feeling, thinking, and interacting also engages with possibilities of both aesthetic and physical development.

How can this multimodal power of the spirit be conceived in social, political, academic, and religious environments? Here the young Hegel, the mastermind of the spirit, offers fruitful insights.

Religion and Spirit: The Fertile Natural Theology of the Young Hegel

"We know that we still cannot say what is really going on in Hegel's thought—the last that was capable of uniting a theory of science, society, consciousness, and world. Although no one doubts its significance, its diagnosis is still outstanding."[18] This 1971 assertion by Dieter Henrich, the leading German-speaking authority on German Idealism, is still valid. Penetrating into the subtler depths of Hegel's excursions into thought, however, and into his demanding theory of the spirit becomes easier if we start with the early writings from Hegel's time as a tutor in Bern (1793–96) and Frankfurt (1797–1801).

For over a century, scholars hardly paid attention to these writings, and it was not until 1907 that they were published, on the initiative of Wilhelm Dilthey.[19] Almost another century passed before an exemplary edition of these writings appeared in two volumes in 1989 and 2014 as part of Hegel's collected works, providing a reliable foundation for better understanding Hegel's early philosophical development. With almost criminological acumen, editors used the changes in Hegel's handwriting and in the watermarks of his manuscript paper in Bern and Frankfurt as a basis for dating with at least some reliability these texts, texts that Hegel variously reworked over time and that were in part also quite fragmentary.

On April 16, 1795, Hegel, twenty-four years old at the time, wrote to his friend Schelling from Bern: "Religion and politics have joined hands in the same underhanded game. The former has taught what despotism willed: contempt for the human race, its incapacity for any good whatsoever, its incapacity to be something on its own."[20] Hegel

18. Dieter Henrich, *Hegel im Kontext* (Frankfurt: Suhrkamp, 1971; new ed. Berlin: Suhrkamp, 2010), 7.

19. G. W. F. Hegel, *Hegels theologische Jugendschriften*, ed. Herman Nohl (Tübingen: Mohr Siebeck, 1907; repr. Verlag der Wissenschaften, 2018). English trans.: G. W. F. Hegel, *Early Theological Writings*, trans. T. M. Knox and Richard Kroner (Philadelphia: University of Pennsylvania Press, 1975, 8th ed., 1996).

20. G. W. F. Hegel, *Hegel: The Letters*, trans. Clark Butler and Christiane Seiler (Bloomington: Indiana University Press, 1984), 35.

expected the further development of the more recent philosophy of freedom (Kant, Fichte) to prove the dignity of humankind, in connection with which he anticipated two consequences: "The aura of prestige surrounding the heads of the oppressors and gods of this earth is disappearing. The philosophers are proving the dignity of man. The peoples will learn to feel it. Not only will they demand their rights, which have been trampled in the dust, they will take them back themselves, they will appropriate them."[21]

Over the following months in Bern, from May 5, 1795, to July 24, 1795, Hegel worked on a text that was not published until 1907, under the title *The Life of Jesus*.[22] Hegel himself was apparently not particularly proud of this early piece, for in a letter on August 30, 1795, to his admired friend Schelling, who was already publishing quite sophisticated speculative philosophical texts, he did not even mention these studies. And indeed, at first glance Hegel's text seems to be merely a "gospel harmony" in which he "relates the life of Jesus in simple words," thus the description given by the editors of the popular German paperback edition of his works in twenty volumes.[23] Those editors remark further that although this piece is certainly of significance as the "only completely preserved work from Hegel's time in Bern, it is nonetheless of little significance for Hegel's philosophical development,"[24] an opinion prompting them not to include it in the paperback edition.

21. Hegel, *The Letters*, 35.

22. G. W. F. Hegel, *Three Essays, 1793–1795: The Tubingen Essay, Berne Fragments, The Life of Jesus*, trans. Peter Fuss and John Dobbins (Notre Dame: University of Notre Dame Press, 1984), 104–65; https://www.scribd.com/document/227694655/Life-of-Jesus-Das -Leben-Jesu-G-W-F-Hegel.

23. G. W. F. Hegel, *Frühe Schriften, Werke 1,* Theorie Werkausgabe (Frankfurt: Suhrkamp Verlag, 1971), 622.

24. Hegel, *Frühe Schriften, Werke 1*, 622.

Yet anyone who follows the development of Hegel's early writings cannot but come to a quite different conclusion. In 1793 Kant's influential book *Religion within the Boundaries of Mere Reason* had been published. Hegel had read this piece attentively and now incorporated Kant's findings into his own studies on the life of Jesus, combining New Testament religiosity focused on Jesus with the more prominent philosophical ideas of his age in the field of ethics. Hegel maintains that considerable credit is due Christ for "his recognition of genuine morality, and for his purer worship of God."[25] Jesus allegedly promoted "reason's light, for it imposes morality as a matter of duty"; praised "reason's tribunal," which every person should approach through "self-knowledge"; and extolled the "spirit of the rational world," which is nothing less than the "spirit of divinity."[26]

Reason and the law of reason; ethics and the law of ethics; duty, virtue, and dignity; morality and the inner law of freedom—Hegel's *Life of Jesus* is replete with the ideas and terminology of Kant and of popular interpretations of Kantian ethics. He emphasizes "man's dignity and his capacity to derive from his own self the concept of divinity and the comprehension of the divine will."[27] In this sense, Jesus's proclamation of the reign of God wholly corresponds to Kant's explications in his piece on religion.[28] He taught "belief in the sacred law of your own reason"[29] and in the indwelling "holy spirit of virtue."[30]

25. Hegel, *Three Essays*, 104.

26. Hegel, *Three Essays*, 108–9.

27. Hegel, *Three Essays*, 118.

28. The reference is to the proclamation of "God's kingdom purely as a realm of goodness, one in which reason and law alone govern" (Hegel, *Three Essays*, 129).

29. Hegel, *Three Essays*, 148.

30. Hegel, *Three Essays*, 134. Hegel is also interested in Jesus's disputes with the Jews, particularly with Pharisaic religiosity and

This text from Hegel's sojourn in Bern is not simply a naive side note to his studies at the time. Even in his later studies and reworkings of texts from Bern during his time in Frankfurt, Hegel repeatedly returned to Jesus and his ministry, albeit with different focal points. Although he continued to follow the lofty speculative works of Fichte and Schelling, he now focused primarily on the variously radiating influence of religion on general morality and politics in the power of the spirit. His burning question was: How can a spirit of freedom be evoked and spread among people by philosophically and morally educated religion or by religiously informed philosophy?

In his text "Positivity of the Christian Religion," dated September 24, 1800, he emphasizes the power of the Christian religion to shape different political considerations in history and even to bridge social differences and tensions, appropriately observing that severely oppressed people and their overlords attended one church.[31]

Criticizing the enlightened critique of religion, Hegel insists "that the convictions of many centuries represented in dogmatic Christianity, regarded as sacrosanct, true, and obligatory by the millions who lived and died by them in those centuries, were not, at least on their subjective side,

---

morality. However, he depicts their positions against the standard of Kantian ethics in condescending clichés. Nonetheless, Hegel does allow his Jesus to remark to "several Greek Jews" that "if they but obey the sacred law of their reason, then we are brothers—members of one and the same society" (147–48).

31. "It was the religion of the Italian states in the finest period of their licentious freedom in the Middle Ages; of the grave and free Swiss republics; of the more or less moderate monarchies of modern Europe; alike of the most heavily oppressed serfs and their overlords: both attended one church." Friedrich [sic] Hegel, *On Christianity: Early Theological Writings*, trans. T. M. Knox and Richard Kroner (New York: Harper Torchbooks, 1961), 168; see also 67–181.

downright folly or plain immorality."[32] He sees it as the task of theologically sophisticated philosophy to disclose what exactly deserves to be called the divine Spirit.[33] Over against negative critiques of religion after the fashion of the Enlightenment, he remarks critically: "If reason fixes its eye on the transient element alone and cries out about superstition, then reason is to blame for setting to work superficially and overlooking the eternal."[34]

Despite his respect for metaphysical considerations of the relationship between the finite and the infinite among his friends and contemporaries, Hegel is not really interested simply in engaging in metaphysics. His studies intend instead to enhance our discernment of the religiously, morally, and politically radiating presence of what he calls the spirit of life, a moral and political entity. That is, he intends to explore the religious and moral-political presence of a spirit, "a Being who transcends our consciousness of human agency." The divine Spirit should become "the animating spirit of human life."[35]

In fragments from September 1800, Hegel polemicizes against his philosophical colleagues and their inclination to turn the relationship between the finite and the infinite into a product of mere reflection.[36] He similarly objects to Fichte's positing of an absolute I—that is, "a phenomenon of the time, at bottom equivalent to the phenomenon of dependence on an absolutely alien being which cannot become man."[37]

Not only a metaphysical theology of a transcendent God but also a speculative philosophy of the absolute

32. Hegel, *Three Essays*, 172.
33. Cf. Hegel, *On Christianity*, 176.
34. Hegel, *Three Essays*, 177.
35. Hegel, *On Christianity*, 176.
36. Hegel, *Three Essays*, 153.
37. Hegel, *On Christianity*, 318–19.

I or the absolute subject must be rejected. Both forms are equally alienating and present no paths of freedom and elevation. Hegel understands "spirit" as "the living unity of the manifold."[38] He finds this spirit at work as a living unity of multiplicity in moral and political arrangements based on freedom[39] and is keenly interested in the conflicts such entities have with oppressive religious and political powers.

The spirit is a living, integrative power within human subjectivity and the latter's varied mental faculties as well as within the religious, moral, and political spheres of life. As such, the spirit manifests itself in various forms amid ever-changing cultural and historical surroundings. Although Hegel's understanding of the spirit acquires considerable sophistication and architectural beauty in his mature philosophy, it also suffers severe losses. In Jena, Hegel would go on to publish his *Phenomenology of Spirit*.[40] He would clarify differences between his own philosophy and that of leading philosophers of his age.[41] And finally

38. Hegel, *On Christianity*, 311.

39. See the "Fragmente einer Kritik der Verfassung Deutschlands" that date as far back as Hegel's time in Frankfurt (in G. W. F. Hegel, *Gesammelte Werke*, vol. 5, *Schriften und Entwürfe (1799–1808)*, ed. Manfred Baum and Kurt Rainer Meist [Hamburg: Felix Meiner, 1998], 1–24).

40. G. W. F. Hegel, *Phänomenologie des Geistes*, vol. 9 of *Gesammelte Werke*, ed. Wolfgang Bonsiepen and Reinhard Heede (Hamburg: Felix Meiner, 1980); English trans.: *The Phenomenology of Spirit*, trans. Terry Pinkard (Cambridge: Cambridge University Press, 2019).

41. Hegel, "Differenz des Fichte'schen und Schelling'schen Systems der Philosophie," in G. W. F. Hegel, *Jenaer Kritische Schriften*, vol. 4 of *Gesammelte Werke*, ed. Hartmut Buchner and Otto Pöggeler (Hamburg: Felix Meiner, 1968), 1–92; Hegel, "Glauben und Wissen," in Hegel, *Jenaer Kritische Schriften*, 313–414.

he would also enter into the competition to optimize the study of transcendental philosophy and metaphysics. Even then, however, continuity with his early ideas and visions is clearly discernible.

For Hegel's later development continued to be shaped by an understanding of the spirit influenced by distinctly Christian religiosity; by a reflection on the connective powers of religion, politics, and philosophy in their reactionary, in their liberal, and in their revolutionary forms; and by a consciousness of the cultural and historical polymorphism of the spirit.

Hegel's understanding of the spirit, however, became problematic when he integrated metaphysical and totalizing figures and forms of thought into his philosophy. While on this basis right-wing Hegelians and others praised this philosopher of the *Weltgeist*, admirer of Aristotle, and defender of classical metaphysics and even attributed to him an interest in a "cosmic spirit,"[42] left-wing Hegelians (Feuerbach, Ruge, Moses Heß, Karl Marx) who had welcomed Hegel's youthful passion for freedom could not go along with this development because it threatened the spirit of freedom in society. They regarded the older Hegel as a servant of an authoritarian state, a state that he even saw as the manifest God.[43]

42. See also Charles Taylor, *Hegel* (Cambridge, MA: Cambridge University Press, 1975), with impacts on his own theory of the self and his cultural analysis.

43. "The state consists in the march of God in the world, and its basis is the power of reason actualizing itself as will." G. W. F. Hegel, *Elements of the Philosophy of Right*, ed. Allen W. Wood, trans. H. B. Nisbet (Cambridge: Cambridge University Press, 1991), 279 (§258); "But we must not for a moment imagine that the physical world of nature is of a higher order than the world of the spirit; for the state is as far above physical life as spirit is above nature. We should therefore venerate the state as an earthly divinity" (307 [§272]).

It is the early dynamics of Hegel's thinking that provide the proper lens through which to perceive and appreciate the richness of his theory of the spirit and its fruitful impulses even for today. His expansive lectures on the philosophy of religion, the philosophy of history, the history of philosophy, and the basic outlines of the philosophy of law all richly attest this consistent focus on a multimodal spirit, operative not only in human minds but also in a multitude of historical and cultural environments.

In the following lectures I will explore how divine and human multimodal spirits gain contours in their work for justice, for freedom, for truth, and for peace. They constitute powerful counterforces against the human misery, self-endangerment, and brutality addressed in the first of my lectures on the image of God.

*[handwritten marginal note: * If divine Spirit = God's active creativity, these dispersed ideas gain some integrity]*

Lecture 3

CALLED TO JUSTICE

A Social State and a State Governed by the Rule of Law

Emerging from the horrors of the National Socialist reign of terror and from the widespread devastation initiated by the Germans in the Second World War, Germany turned its attention to establishing a new domestic political organization and thereby also a path back to international respectability. In the western part of the divided country, the constitutional draft of the Federal Republic chose the self-designation of a "social state governed by the rule of law" (article 28, paragraph 1, sentence 1).[1]

The designation "governed by the rule of law" involves the self-obligation to create universally binding laws and to tie the actions of all state organs to this constitution and these laws. The designation "social state" expresses the political self-obligation to secure social justice and security for all citizens (that is, balanced social equality) and to support the disadvantaged and those otherwise in need of protection.

1. Basic Law for the Federal Republic of Germany in the revised version published in the Federal Law Gazette Part III, classification number 100–1, as last amended by Article 1 of the Act of March 28, 2019 (Federal Law Gazette I, 404).

The goal of this double designation "social state" and "state governed by the rule of law" was to address and solve politically an extremely difficult problem—namely, securing justice in a complex polity while adhering to a vision of justice that essentially means the *freedom and equality of all people*. Such politically and legally secured equal treatment of all people before the law and before legal authorities along with the accompanying equal rights of men, women, and social minorities in public life evolved into a universal ethos of equality and a universal promise of freedom. The foundation for this principle is the United Nations Human Rights Convention of 1948, which states: "All human beings are born free and equal in dignity and rights. They are endowed with reason and conscience and should act towards one another in a spirit of brotherhood."[2]

The polity, however, encounters enormous formative problems insofar as concrete human beings living concrete lives have access to extremely *unequal* life and developmental circumstances and to extremely *unequal* possibilities for implementing their freedom. The question becomes how these formative problems can be addressed in a way that adjusts, in a balanced fashion, equal opportunities for all members of society rather than continually repeating or even reinforcing concrete experiences of inequality and curtailed freedom regarding access to material and intellectual goods.

This principle of a "social state governed by the rule of law" constitutes an initial but crucial framework within which the multimodal formative potential of the spirit can come to bear in working toward social circumstances that

2. "United Nations Universal Declaration of Human Rights," article 1; see https://www.un.org/en/universal-declaration-human-rights/.

merit being called "just." In postwar Germany, this framework was supported by a renewal of moral resources and of religious circumstances and educational initiatives.[3] The combination of the rule of law and protection of the weak provides two intellectual and institutional visions of development. First, the legal framework must develop as a humane set of laws that excludes neither persons nor groups on the alleged "periphery" of society. Such a corpus of laws, however, must understand that a commitment to justice involves more than creating laws commensurate with justice, and it is here that the orientation toward protection of the weak discloses creative developmental possibilities for the evolution of law.

The legal encoding of the protection of the weak, moreover, prevents a society from simply making do with the admittedly kind and valuable willingness to help exhibited by individuals and groups. That is, the protection of the weak must be institutionally integrated, legally secured, and universally accepted and expected in complex communities well beyond the simple ethos of concern for one's fellow citizen.

In the practice of law, this rigorous orientation toward the protection of the weak addresses a paradox that confronts all legal and moral developments. What is at work here? People and social institutions are intent on developing and improving their legal rights and modes of moral communication. But how can they address this difficult but indispensable task without endangering or even losing the normative binding power of law and morality? After all,

3. Concerning the carefully planned (in the United States) and then successfully implemented "reeducation" of the Germans, see the excellent study by Heike Springhart, *Aufbrüche zu neuen Ufern: Der Beitrag von Religion und Kirche für Demokratisierung und Reeducation im Westen Deutschlands nach 1945* (Leipzig: EVA, 2008).

law and morality must elicit confidence in all their operations—that is, must insist on reliable, enduring validity. Here the combination of the rule of law with an ethos of protecting the weak proves beneficial in providing energy and stability in the development of just law.

Justice and the Protection of the Weak: A Millennia-Old Ethos

A "social state governed by the rule of law"—by committing to this particular twofold self-obligation in its search for a new political, legal, and moral beginning after 1945, Germany joined a long and grand tradition. For many people in the Christian West, this combination of law and mercy, justice and institutionalized protection of the weak evokes familiar biblical traditions that present God as just and merciful and in turn expect human beings as the "image of God" similarly to exercise justice and provide help for the needy and the weak.[4] And we find this combination of law and protection of the weak not just in Judaism and Christianity but also in other religions and secular writings. Natural theology might well take note that this combination was politically documented over four thousand years ago in a fashion that comes across not only as morally sympathetic and humane but also as significant for any establishment of political loyalty and an efficient legal culture.

Well over four thousand years ago, the Sumerian ruler Urukagina (who reigned ca. 2350 BCE) declared that he had brought peace to the city of Lagash—one of the oldest cities in the Near East, northwest of the conjunction of

4. See Taylor, *Sources of the Self*, 410.

the Euphrates and Tigris Rivers—by becoming an advocate for widows and orphans. That is, here the ruler himself interceded on behalf of the weak in general and of widows and orphans in particular. Urukagina fought against the exploitation of the economically weak by the strong and liberated the town's inhabitants from debt bondage. His self-designation as the protector of widows and orphans apparently procured for him the political loyalty even of those not specifically threatened at the time by poverty or other distress and created thus a climate of peace for all.[5]

The legal texts of Ur-Nammu, king of Ur, the oldest known legal corpus (ca. 2100 BCE), propagated the protection of the weak even in its prologue.[6] The prologue to the Code of Hammurabi, the emblematic legal code of Mesopotamian civilization (dating to ca. eighteenth century BCE), states that "Hammurabi, the devout, god-fearing prince," was chosen to "cause justice to prevail in the land . . . that the strong might not oppress the weak." The epilogue repeats this theme and explicitly associates it with the protection of "the orphan and the widow."[7]

The Old and the New Testaments then incorporate this thematic protection of widows and orphans from neglect,

5. Cf. Michael Aulfinger, *Urukagina, der gerechte König* (Neckenmarkt: Edition Nove, 2007).

6. See F. Ch. Fensham, "Widow, Orphan, and the Poor in Ancient Near Eastern Legal and Wisdom Literature," *Journal of Near Eastern Studies* 21 (1962): 129–39; Jan Assmann, *Ma'at: Gerechtigkeit und Unsterblichkeit im Alten Ägypten* (Munich: Beck, 1990), 245–52. See also James B. Pritchard, ed., *Ancient Near Eastern Texts Relating to the Old Testament*, 3rd ed. (Princeton: Princeton University Press, 1969), 524.

7. *Codex Hammurabi*, trans. Theophile J. Meek, in Pritchard, *Ancient Near Eastern Texts*, 164, 178.

oppression, and exploitation into their own texts almost as a foundational leitmotif and universalize it by expanding it to include a large group of *personae miserae*. Legal texts and prophetic admonitions repeatedly enumerate anew such lists of the weak that need not only practical individual and moral help from fellow citizens but also legal, judicial, political, and religious support. These groups include the poor and the needy, the weak and the humble, those who must do without or otherwise suffer from lack, the oppressed and the stricken, the beaten and the miserable,[8] and foreigners and slaves.

The repeated emphasis on widows and orphans discloses a multimodal connection with the spirit of family ethos. To thwart the emergence of various forms of injustice and radical inequality with respect to developmental possibilities and life circumstances, the underlying theoretical framework of the social state and state governed by the rule of law must refer back to plausible considerations of long-standing family circumstances. To wit, at the beginning of life all human beings are helpless strangers in the world and as such profoundly dependent on care and

---

8. See Bernd Janowski, *Anthropologie des Alten Testaments: Grundlagen—Kontexte—Themenfelder* (Tübingen: Mohr Siebeck, 2019), 252–53; Michael Welker, "Justice—Mercy—Worship: The 'Weighty Matters' of the Biblical Law," in *Concepts of Law in the Sciences, Legal Studies, and Theology*, ed. Michael Welker and Gregor Etzelmüller (Tübingen: Mohr Siebeck, 2013), 205–24; Michael Welker, "The Power of Mercy in Biblical Law," *Journal of Law and Religion* 29, no. 2 (2014): 225–35; Jürgen Moltmann, *Sun of Righteousness, Arise!: God's Future for Humanity and the Earth* (Minneapolis: Fortress, 2010), part 3; Piet Naudé, *Pathways in Ethics: Justice—Interpretation—Discourse—Economics* (Stellenbosch: Sun Media, 2016), part 1; Dirk J. Smit, "'Hope for Even the Most Wretched'? On Remembering the Reformation," *Stellenbosch Theological Journal* 4, no. 2 (2018): 703–25.

support; indeed, most will occasionally experience similar helplessness and dependence again at some time in life and then also, as a rule, at the end of life. In this sense, a universal praxis and commitment to the protection of the weak is clearly associated with family ethos, and it is precisely these experiences that provide a point of contact for a radical ethos of equality.

That said, an element of skepticism has emerged today over against the notion that such family ethos is capable of supporting the spirit of justice. Such skepticism derives from the observation that the continued development of family ethos is still severely restricted by powerful patriarchal and gerontocratic traditions and by tenaciously global nonegalitarian practices hostile to freedom. Judith Butler[9] and others suggest that given the inclination often accompanying traditional family ethos to stigmatize persons and lifestyles that deviate from heterosexual marital and reproductive traditions, perhaps we best not draw too heavily from family ethos as such when trying to promote the spirit of justice and mercy and its institutionalization.

Nonetheless, encouraging efforts have been made to reconcile the traditional concepts of family with modern modes of freedom without entirely surrendering the formative power of family ethos in law and politics.[10] At the same time, drastic changes to the stability traditionally associated with small families and a weakening of the classic connection between religious and family ethos have increasingly prompted many people today to trust other,

9. Butler, *Bodies That Matter*, and her 2018 Gifford Lectures in Glasgow, "My Life, Your Life: Equality and the Philosophy of Non-Violence," https://www.giffordlectures.org/lecturers/judith-butler-0.

10. John Witte Jr., *Church, State, and Family: Reconciling Traditional Teachings and Modern Liberties* (Cambridge: Cambridge University Press, 2019).

different formative powers. An attractive alternative in this sense is an ethos of liberation and social transformation through legal means, a notion that thinkers in antiquity similarly conceived in a visionary fashion.

It is immediately obvious that laws must identify and manage instances of acute conflict, that they must counter any escalation of violence and counterviolence, and that they must provide varied forms of conflict limitation and prophylaxis. Conflict limitation alone, however, is still far from an effective rule of law. After all, conflict limitation can also be attained through calculated intimidation. A culture based on the rule of law is attainable only through institutional articulation of conflict types and the careful incorporation of such types into a schema that can be brought to bear to include and comprehend other cases of conflict.

The point is not to recall past conflicts merely to evoke interest and concern with respect to individual crises and to treat narratively and imaginatively the way concrete crises are woven and tied into various life circumstances. Legal thinking instead isolates and treats past and recent conflicts as self-enclosed, limited cases that can be articulated as *types* according to fixed rules. Here we encounter one of the grand accomplishments of jurisprudence. By comprehending concrete conflicts as legal types, one can by and large already anticipate their resolution and ending. They can be treated as soluble problems—that is, as what in principle resemble resolved conflicts.[11]

One genuinely revolutionary insight that opens up new perspectives and potential for law and the push for

---

11. See Michael Welker, "Security of Expectations: Reformulating the Theology of Law and Gospel," *Journal of Religion* 66 (1986): 237–60.

justice is that even enduring politically, legally, and economically fixed circumstances of radical social inequality can be treated as acute conflicts. One excellent example is what is known as the slave law in the Old Testament as attested in two biblical legal collections: Exodus 21:2–11 and Deuteronomy 15:12–13. The first elementary tenet of this law stipulates that "when you buy a male Hebrew slave, he shall serve six years, but in the seventh he shall go out a free person, without debt [i.e., payment]" (Exod. 21:2).

This slave law is revolutionary in several respects:

- It elevates the fundamental institution of slave-holding, which in ancient societies was an unquestioned and indispensable part of the economic and social order, into a conflict and problem subject to regulation.
- It further defines slaves, who, for example, in Rome were viewed merely as "tools with the power of speech" (Marcus Terentius Varro), as potentially free human beings to be protected even during their lives in slavery.
- And finally, the law itself transcends its function as an instrument of acute conflict management insofar as it now also regulates long-term processes of social transformation—here, for example, the termination of slavery after six years.

Similar to a family ethos that promotes the quest for unconditional human equality and freedom, however, so also is law as a liberating power of social transformation quite ambivalent. For these biblical legal collections merely limit slavery temporally rather than abolish it permanently. And although this limitation does indeed represent humane progress (for the slave is at least potentially a free person and as such deserving of protection), it is still worlds removed from the universal ethos of justice in freedom and equality for which we today strive. And although opposition to slavery dragged on for centuries before achieving modest successes, at least no state today would risk legally sanctioning the enslavement of human beings. The Universal Declaration of Human Rights declares in article 4 that "no one shall be held in slavery or servitude; slavery and the slave trade shall be prohibited in all their forms." Yet even today, more than forty million people still live in conditions of slavery and forced labor.[12]

Hence while one must certainly acknowledge that transformative legal developments do contribute at least modestly to the emergence of circumstances conducive to freedom and equality, such developments are clearly excessively tedious and tend to drag on unnecessarily or even be obscured. Surprisingly, perhaps, much-extolled natural law has contributed to this situation and for centuries has tended to impede the creation of just social circumstances.

The Grand Promises and Miseries of Natural Law[13]

Politically and morally difficult or foundering situations have repeatedly prompted cries for a "return to natural

12. See United Nations, "Universal Declaration of Human Rights," https://www.un.org/en/universal-declaration-human-rights/ and the Global Slavery Index, https://www.globalslaveryindex.org/.

13. This section draws from ideas originally presented in my Heidelberg farewell lecture, "God's Justice and Righteousness," in *Responsibility and the Enhancement of Life: Essays in Honor of William Schweiker*, ed. Günter Thomas and Heike Springhart (Leipzig: EVA, 2017), 179–90.

law." The inevitable waning of initial hopes, however, then similarly issues in laments over the loss of precisely this point of orientation.[14] In his well-known dialogue with Jürgen Habermas, Joseph Cardinal Ratzinger found, on the one hand, that "natural law has remained (especially in the Catholic Church) the key issue in dialogues with secular society and with other communities of faith in order to appeal to the reason we share in common and to seek the basis for a consensus about the ethical principles of law in a secular, pluralistic society."[15] On the other hand, Ratzinger had to concede that "this instrument has become blunt," indeed that the "victory of the theory of evolution has meant the end of this view of nature."[16] It is not, however, the "victory of the theory of evolution" but rather the deficient systematic tenability of the association between nature, on the one hand, and law that takes its orientation from justice, on the other, that has deflated and indeed continues to deflate any hope that this instrument might take us further in the question of how one might more enduringly establish justice and righteousness.[17]

14. Cf. Rudolf Weiler, ed., *Die Wiederkehr des Naturrechts und die Neuevangelisierung Europas* (Vienna: Verlag für Geschichte und Politik, Oldenbourg Verlag, 2005); see also the critical reaction of Ingolf Dalferth, *Naturrecht in protestantischer Perspektive*, Würzburger Vorträge zur Rechtsphilosophie, Rechtstheorie und Rechtssoziologie 38 (Baden-Baden: Nomos, 2008). Cf. also Welker and Etzelmüller, *Concepts of Law*.

15. Joseph Ratzinger, "What Keeps the World Together," in Jürgen Habermas and Joseph Ratzinger, *Dialectics of Secularization: On Reason and Religion*, ed. Florian Schuller, trans. Brian McNeil (San Francisco: Ignatius, 2006), 69.

16. Ratzinger, "What Keeps the World Together." See in this regard Michael Welker, "Habermas and Ratzinger on the Future of Religion," *Scottish Journal of Theology* 63, no. 4 (2010): 456–73.

17. John Witte Jr. has suggested that, given its long and largely

Natural law obscures a fact most people prefer to ignore—namely, that all life lives at the cost of other life. The mathematician and philosopher Alfred North Whitehead repeatedly addressed this theme, articulating it quite succinctly in the assertion that life is robbery; it lives at the cost of other life.[18] Nature does, it is true, exhibit a high degree of effective organization, fruitfulness, and beauty. It surprises and delights through powers of regeneration and renewal. Every blooming flower, every childbirth, every dawn, every reemergence of spring is capable of eliciting surprise and delight. But natural earthly life also exhibits the ineluctable cruelty of life at the cost of other life. Even vegetarians must destroy life to nourish themselves. Hence any unqualified references to nature and life as salvific concepts, or certainly any equating of God and nature, are naive and carelessly considered. Those wishing to avoid living under perpetual legal, moral, and religious illusions, those striving for theological sincerity with respect to creation, must ask for an understanding of justice that acknowledges this profound ambivalence attaching to natural life.

This systematic foundering of references to natural law is already evident in the classical collection of Roman law, the *Corpus Iuris Civilis*, published in 529. Its initial section, *Institutiones*, subdivides private law into "the natural law," "the law of nations," and "the civil law."[19] In 533 the east-

---

well-intentioned history, we should tolerate the metaphorical use of the natural-law rhetoric. See also his impressive contribution "Law, Religion, and Metaphors," in *Risiko und Vertrauen = Risk and Trust: Festschrift für Michael Welker zum 70. Geburtstag,* ed. H. Springhart and G. Thomas (Leipzig: EVA, 2017), 177–94.

18. Whitehead, *Process and Reality*, 105.

19. *The Institutes of Justinian*, in *The Roman World*, vol. 3 of *The Library of Original Sources*, ed. Oliver J. Thatcher (Milwaukee: University Research Extension, 1907), 100.

ern Roman emperor, Justinian, legally sanctioned this doctrine—"in the name of our Lord Jesus Christ."

In this view, natural law is "that law which nature
teaches to all animals. For this law does not belong exclusively to the human race, but belongs to all animals,
whether of the earth, the air, or the water. Hence comes
the union of the male and female, which we term mat-
rimony; hence the procreation and bringing up of children."[20] That is, the fundamental formative element here
is family ethos. With respect to the alleged breadth of
validity of natural law, however, the *Corpus Iuris Civilis*
maintains that jurisprudence is not only the "science of
the just and the unjust" but also "the knowledge of things
divine and human."[21]

The problems raised by associating natural law with
justice and righteousness become clear the moment we
no longer restrict our discussion merely to loving family
relationships. The introduction to the *Institutiones* states
that "the maxims of law are these: to live honestly, to hurt
no one, to give every one his due."[22] The commandment
"to hurt no one" is indeed quite difficult to apply to "all
animals, whether of the earth, the air, or the water." The
moment one accepts what is known as the "law of the
strongest" as "natural law," the commandment to "give every one his due" quite loses the aura implying that it somehow still involves justice and righteousness. The National
Socialists, as is well known, positioned this expression—*To
Every One His Due*—cruelly and cynically over the main
gate of the Buchenwald concentration camp, legible,
moreover, from the inside.

20. *The Institutes of Justinian*, 100–101.
21. *The Institutes of Justinian*, 100.
22. *The Institutes of Justinian*, 100.

Paolo Prodi's history of justice claims to reconstruct "how the concept of justice has been lived and conceived in our Western culture." Although this book's German translation bears the subtitle "Vom Recht Gottes zum modernen Rechtsstaat"—that is, "from God's law to the modern state under the rule of laws"[23]—references to God's justice, divine law, and God's righteousness are remarkably pale and vague in all of the book's sources and interpretive discussions. The guiding perspective focuses on the correlation between the cosmic and natural and the political and legal organization of life circumstances, conditions, and relationships. Divine law in connection with natural law is assigned the role of guaranteeing the normatively binding character of laws and their just disposition.

In his book, Prodi traces the perpetually shifting coalitions of divine law, natural law, cosmic and natural regularities, and also of the various political and legal concepts of organization and implementation over the course of Western history. In their own turn, these perpetually shifting configurations have been accompanied by the constantly shifting dominance of various ecclesiastical, theological, political, legal, and philosophical institutions and thinkers. Martin Luther's laconic dictum that "we prattle on a great deal about natural law" (*De lege naturae multa fabulamur*)[24] is trenchantly confirmed by the history of the development and reception of this notion of natural law, which has ultimately functioned as a carousel for changing orientational claims and arrogations of power.[25]

23. Paolo Prodi, *Eine Geschichte der Gerechtigkeit: Vom Recht Gottes zum modernen Rechtsstaat* (Munich: Beck, 2005).

24. Martin Luther, *Werke, Kritische Gesamtausgabe*, vol. 56 (Weimar: Böhlau, 1938), 355, 14.

25. The ambivalent and brutal aspects of nature are blurred by references to the caring family in all living species. The impression

In modernity's concentration on this theme, it is then the human spirit, human reason, and human conscience that acquire increasing significance. We hear more and more frequently that natural law in fact resides in the human mind and reason itself. The notions of individual conscience and moral communication now become important players in the multifarious conflicts between obedience to divine law, national law, the prince's commands, and positive law. What ultimately emerges is that, on the one hand, conscience and positive law are emancipated from religion, and, on the other, conscience as the inner judge, often in the name of God, is polarized over against professional judges acting in the name of society. But does reference to natural law and to divine and human justice and righteousness not degenerate here into ciphers intended merely to underscore and reinforce the subjective sensibility and feeling for morality and justice along with the status quo of social power relations?

The Multimodal Spirit of Justice

Is it not utterly discouraging to realize that references to natural law can be so unreliable or even deceptive as a foundation for justice? For on what basis, then, are we to establish and defend human equality and freedom? Radically skeptical philosophy suggests dispensing entirely with natural law before comprehensively reevaluating *all* our legal, political, and moral preconceptions. As the philosopher Rüdiger Bittner observes, "We have long been accustomed to understanding our behavior, and especially our political

---

of stability and predictability accompanying this "law" derives from natural and cosmic powers.

behavior, as being subject to a higher authority, for example, to natural law, divine law, the notion of human rights, and so on, however such authority be conceived. And the realization that in reality these really amount to nothing can be profoundly disturbing. But it need not be."[26]

Bittner proposes a modest retreat to personal experience, human prudence, and educational training that rigorously dispenses with not only religious but also grand political, legal, and moral concepts and orientational expectations. Following and even intensifying the radical philosophical critiques of religion presented by the classical philosophers Feuerbach, Marx, and Nietzsche, he also radically questions the efficacy of this lofty conceptual world with respect to legal and political thinking and action. The proclamation of universal human dignity, Bittner maintains, has utterly failed to establish a sheltering aura around the life of each individual human being.[27]

But is it genuinely *only* through radical ethical skepticism that we can come to terms with this loss of faith in natural law? I am suggesting in these lectures that we adopt and trust in the power of a multimodal spirit of the sort already evident in numerous historical and empirical contexts. For the synthesizing and differentiating power of the spirit is already at work in myriad processes of cognitive, moral, and aesthetic perception and communication. This power cannot, however, be reduced merely to some human mental faculty, regardless of how mighty one may conceive such to be. It is neither "nature" nor "culture" but rather a plethora of natural and cultural circumstances and

26. Rüdiger Bittner, *Bürger sein: Eine Prüfung politischer Begriffe* (Munich: de Gruyter, 2017), 144.
27. Rüdiger Bittner, "Without Laws," in Welker and Etzelmüller, *Concepts of Law*, 339–53.

events that shape and sustain human mental operations that in their own turn are thereby also shaped and developed further. As operations of the spirit, these human processes are also inherently inclined toward completion and perfection, though in individual cases such an inclination can be quite modest or even dull.

And yet the more modest steadying tendencies of intellectual life should not seduce one into underestimating the powerful creativity of the spirit. Here we must note those particular multimodal spiritual interrelations within legal culture, political culture, family ethos, and the ethos of social innovation that have been developed and indeed thoroughly tested for millennia and that constantly interact with human cognitive, moral, and aesthetic faculties. Hence it is bold but by no means absurd to proclaim and work toward a universal ethos and praxis of human dignity, human rights, and justice in the sense of the freedom and equality of all human beings.

Of course, neither lofty but naively expansive claims ("nature demands," "culture intends") nor hectic searches for saving principles suffice here. It is instead imperative for us to discover and foster processes of mutual ethical support in both natural and cultural spheres—as long as they are open to being shaped anew by the human spirit. The rule of law, politics, and the intellectual connections between the two are indispensable in the quest for justice. However, the development of their full potential requires that other forces come into play as well. Such include impulses from the spheres of family ethos and social-civil ethos that seek to limit forces hostile to freedom and support those that favor liberation. And these forces in their own turn ideally derive from a spectrum of empathy that fosters a committed culture of compassionate helping and an unwavering focus on the freedom and equality of all.

This expansive spectrum of empathy, however, offers the most varied possibilities for engagement—ranging from a simple expression of sympathy ("I'm so sorry you are not doing well"), to personal engagement and organized aid, all the way to the lifelong commitment of the entirety of one's energies to helping the weak and disadvantaged. In her 1992 Edinburgh Gifford Lectures, "Upheavals of Thought: A Theory of Emotions,"[28] Martha Nussbaum collected and assessed a wealth of personal emotions of dismayed distress and interpersonal sympathy—gleaned from both literature and philosophical reflection and deriving from both private and public life—including compassion, empathy, altruism, benevolence, sympathy, mercy, pity, partiality, concern, and grief.

This collection provides a mighty emotional reservoir of terms for articulating both individual and shared feelings and emotions as well as moral and social processes of communication. This emotional-moral reservoir represents an indispensable source and foundation for legal, political, medical, scholarly, and educational strategies for developing and enhancing an ethos of justice, equality, and freedom. This moral resource is especially discernible in those grand figures committed to the protection of the weak and the nonviolent struggle for justice and egalitarian freedom, figures whose exemplary lives have become an indelible part of international cultural memory. Even during their lifetimes, Albert Schweitzer, Martin Luther King Jr., and Mother Teresa were honored by the bestowal of the Nobel Peace Prize.

In what way, however, does religion strengthen these

28. Published as Martha C. Nussbaum, *Upheavals of Thought: The Intelligence of Emotions* (Cambridge: Cambridge University Press, 2001); concerning the following discussion, see 297–454.

ethical emotional resources and sustain those models in their pursuit of justice? By focusing on God's vision of human beings—and thus of me as well—religion expands its vision to include the entire breadth of human existence together with the commonalities and similarities of all human beings and the accompanying potential power. From the perspective of each individual, concrete situation, we human beings are unique and unalike. But this perspective changes once we engage in a kind of slow-motion view—that is, when we take note of the children, the sick, the weak, and the elderly not only *among* us but *within* us.

Without denying our concrete bodily existence, we are able to imagine our own existence in countless other situations with innumerable points of contact and intersections with the ongoing lives of others. Religiously shaped perception and thinking *universalize* a person's otherwise quite individual reality. Indeed, some religious traditions associate this expansion of perception with the ascription of enormous human formative powers. That is, God considers human beings capable of a great deal and thus also expects a great deal from them, for God views them within a long-term perspective far transcending the lives of individuals within any given epoch.

Even legal and political ordinances are viewed against the backdrop of expansive temporal horizons in which God rewards good deeds while also, however, "punishing children for the iniquity of parents, to the third and the fourth generation" (Gen. 50:23; cf. Exod. 20:5; 34:7; Num. 14:18; Deut. 5:9). Legal, political, and moral accomplishments and transgressions are viewed from a perspective far transcending current moral and legal human sensibilities and experiences. The Bible takes careful account of precisely this breadth of human existence and human responsibility in its doctrine of human beings made in the image of God—as *imago Dei*—and accordingly also with respect to what is known as the commission for dominion, the most important documentation for which is Genesis 1:26–28:

> Then God said, "Let us make humankind in our image, according to our likeness; and let them have dominion over the fish of the sea, and over the birds of the air, and over the cattle, and over all the wild animals of the earth, and over every creeping thing that creeps upon the earth."
>
> So God created humankind in his image,
>   in the image of God he created them;
>   male and female he created them.
> God blessed them, and God said to them, "Be fruitful and multiply, and fill the earth and subdue it; and have dominion over the fish of the sea and over the birds of the air and over every living thing that moves upon the earth."

Many interpreters, including prominent voices such as Barth's and Moltmann's, have understood this reference to the image of God as applying to the partnership of man and woman, the relationship of I and Thou, or to peaceful (plural) sociality. They abstracted thereby from any notion of forceful dominion over the earth and the world of animals.[29] Inspired by an influential article by Phyllis Bird,[30] I argued already in my 1991 Princeton Warfield Lectures for what Mark Harris accurately called a "functional account of the *Imago Dei*" in Genesis.[31] Not dialogue and

29. See in this regard my assessment of the positions of Karl Barth and Jürgen Moltmann in Michael Welker, *Creation and Reality* (Minneapolis: Fortress, 1999), 65–69.

30. See Phyllis Bird, "'Male and Female He Created Them': Gen 1:27b in the Context of the Priestly Account of Creation," *Harvard Theological Review* 74 (1981): 129–31, esp. 155.

31. Mark Harris, "The Biblical Text and a Functional Account of

sociability but the practical sustenance of creation is the main point of the "call to dominion." Other interpreters, however, adduce the commission for dominion as biblical support for ecological brutalism. This text does indeed ascribe a privileged position to human beings over against fellow creatures. It even uses verbs associated with subjugation (*RDH* and *KBŠ*) and with the language used to describe conquerors and slaveholders. It thus gives a sober and realistic account of the human species in its relation to fellow creatures that compete for self-sustenance. It does not offer cozy and romantic pictures of an unrealistic harmony of all creatures on earth. (Even good gardeners, an image many people would like to apply to humans, never enter their gardens without pruning instruments.) The text speaks clearly against a destructive ecological brutalism, since even conquerors and slaveholders had to take care of the persons they subjugated. The "mandate of dominion" privileges the position of the human species but simultaneously obligates humans, male and female, to exercise such dominion in a fashion informed by sustaining solicitude and care.[32]

Our own ecologically imperiled age is not the first to lament human failure in the face of this commission, for even witnesses from antiquity document such dismay. And for just that reason, any reference to human beings as the image of God needs constant self-assessment and self-criticism. At the same time, we must remain mindful that human beings, through the divine and the human spirit, have indeed been endowed with the powers necessary for

the *Imago Dei*," in *Finding Ourselves after Darwin: Conversations on the Image of God, Original Sin, and the Problem of Evil,* ed. Stanley Rosenberg (Grand Rapids: Baker Academic, 2018), 48–63.

32. Welker, *Creation and Reality*, 60–73.

living up to this grand destiny. I was convinced by David Fergusson's argument that "the concept of the *imago Dei* is best interpreted as designating a complex identity that is established by a providential ordering of human life." Fergusson proposes a "recourse to a more holistic description that includes functional, relational, and practical elements."[33] And he also proposes to consider moving beyond the much-admired framework of a theology of revelation that we find in David Kelsey's magisterial anthropology. My endeavor to supplement Kelsey's christological and eschatological framing of the *imago* teaching by a natural-theological concentration on the divine Spirit and the human spirit tries to follow this helpful advice.

The multimodal spirit sensitizes people to experiences of justice and mercy in personal, familial, social, and political situations, either through personal experience or through personal engagement in bringing about such experiences. That multimodal spirit focuses especially on interpersonal relationships and is rigorously honest in its view of the privileged status of human beings in the creaturely world. And despite numerous discouraging setbacks, it holds fast—within a polyphony of feelings, experiences, and engagement on behalf of fellow human beings and the weak—to an ethos of justice and equality accompanied by an ethos of freedom, a commitment to truth, and a will to peace. Sanguine patience, a profound sensibility for dignity, though also serene confidence and joy invariably accompany and sustain this activity of the spirit among, through, and beyond living human beings.

33. David Fergusson, "Humans Created according to the IMAGO DEI: An Alternative Proposal," *Zygon* 48 (2013): 440. With respect to "providential ordering," see David Fergusson, *The Providence of God: A Polyphonic Approach* (Cambridge: Cambridge University Press, 2018).

Summary

How can one dispel radical doubts concerning the statement of equality from the United Nations Human Rights Convention of 1948—namely, that "all human beings are born free and equal in dignity and rights"? And not only by social and political realities but also philosophically and ethically? How can an ethos of equality be affirmed if natural law is unable to undergird it?

This lecture suggests a solution from the perspective of a multimodal spirit that cannot, however, be reduced to mere intellect. For this multimodal spirit has for millennia in the spheres of jurisprudence, politics, and morality efficaciously combined the commitment to justice with a commitment to the protection of the weak. This spirit is nourished by various impulses from family ethos, by a broad spectrum of feelings of empathy, and by religious perspectives that direct our attention across multiple generations and toward the grand destiny of human beings—something naturally also discernible in secular contexts. In this capacity, the multimodal spirit provides impetus to the worldwide, peaceful struggle for justice and the resulting edification and elevation of human beings.

Lecture 4

CALLED TO FREEDOM

In the previous lecture, I introduced the notion of the multimodal spirit of justice within the context of Germany and Western culture at large. This context, one definitively shaped by Christianity and the European Enlightenment, defines justice above all as *equality*. But in a world characterized by radically *inequitable* life circumstances—including within Western nations—any institution or individual committed to the principle of equality and the spirit of justice faces a considerable and difficult challenge.

Two conditions must be fulfilled for any just commitment to equality to succeed. First, mutual control between the legal system and politics is essential. That matrix of control, however, must never always emanate from the same source. And second, one must achieve the politically, legally, and morally secured and internally inculcated commitment to the protection of the weaker members of society and to the continuous improvement of society toward more balanced—that is, more equitable—conditions. The requisite empathy for such commitment can derive from emotional and moral resources stimulated by family ethos, religion, and educational institutions, though certainly also by the media and the arts. Furthermore, compulsory schooling and education for children and young people, the most comprehensive health-care provisions possible, and an energetic civil society can nourish and promote a

culture of willing assistance and equal opportunity conducive to a society characterized by justice. At the same
time, however, this culture of willing assistance and commitment to justice should not be allowed to create or per-
petuate dependencies that in their own turn compromise
a recipient's sense of independence or autonomy. Hence
it is indispensable that the multimodal spirit of justice be
joined by the similarly multimodal spirit of freedom.

In the following, I will survey the elementary forms
of this multimodal spirit of freedom before turning to its
moral and political manifestations and, finally, to its relationship with religion.

Elementary Forms of Freedom

The grand concepts of justice, freedom, truth, and peace
elicit equally grand hopes, plans, and expectations. And
indeed, these concepts can function quite well as beneficent stimulants in summoning, shaping, and strengthening
various individual and institutional powers for good, something we saw earlier with respect to the ethos of justice. At
the same time, however, they should continually provoke
critical and self-critical reexamination. To take but a cou-
ple of examples: Do what we generally view as benevolent
family circumstances or the prevailing forms of religion
in our countries *genuinely* promote a spirit of justice and
freedom? How, then, is one to explain—if I may return for
a moment to circumstances in Germany—that a country
whose government is constitutionally bound to ensure a
"social state governed by the rule of law" and to ensure
that the use of property "shall also serve the public good,"[1]

1. German constitution, article 28, paragraph 1, sentence 1, and
article 14, respectively.

and that extols the accomplishments of a "social market economy"[2]—how is it possible that such a country must be told that "nowhere in the entire Eurozone is wealth as unequally distributed as in Germany"?[3] Do such grand slogans not issue instead into mere empty promises or even obfuscate the real state of affairs?

In his comprehensive examination of political concepts, the German philosopher Rüdiger Bittner provides a profoundly skeptical assessment of political references to freedom, human dignity, human rights, justice, and democracy.[4] With respect to the topic of freedom, he suggests refraining from high-flown notions of freedom and making do instead with a minimalistic understanding—namely, that being free means "to be without barriers."[5] Such minimalist thinking first of all makes it quite clear that no person is ever completely and utterly free from boundaries and hindrances. Or as Wolfgang Huber puts it: "Freedom is indeed an illusion if understood as *absolute* freedom, but it is also an illusion to believe one can separate it from the physical conditions of life."[6]

Many people in our world today are in fact largely unfree, oppressed as they are by physical (hunger, crushing

2. Alfred Müller-Armack, *Wirtschaftslenkung und Marktwirtschaft* (Hamburg: Verlag für Wirtschaft und Sozialpolitik, 1947), passim.

3. Quoting Markus Grabka, Deutsches Institut für Wirtschaftsforschung, Berlin, in Wolfgang Kessler, "Wider die gefährliche Spaltung: Warum Deutschland eine gerechtere Verteilung des Reichtums braucht," *Zeitzeichen* 20 (2000): 33.

4. Rüdiger Bittner, *Bürger sein: Eine Prüfung politischer Begriffe* (Munich: de Gruyter, 2017).

5. Bittner, *Bürger sein*, 22–23; see Rüdiger Bittner, "What It Is to Be Free," in *Quests for Freedom: Biblical, Historical, Contemporary*, 2nd ed., ed. Michael Welker (Eugene, OR: Wipf & Stock, 2019), 114.

6. Wolfgang Huber, *Ethik: Grundfragen unseres Lebens* (Munich: Beck, 2013), 13.

poverty, chronic illnesses) and spiritual (fear, persecution, terror) distress. Hannah Arendt trenchantly articulated this state of affairs as follows: "Only those who know freedom from want can appreciate fully the meaning of freedom from fear, and only those who are free from both want and fear are in a position to conceive a passion for public freedom, to develop within themselves that *goût* or taste for *liberté* and the peculiar taste for *égalité* or equality that *liberté* carries within it."[7]

But it is not just those living in distress and fear who enjoy hardly any freedoms but also those who, though indeed living in environments allowing a person to live largely free of distress and fear, have nonetheless maneuvered themselves into situations of acute lack of freedom as a result of, for example, addiction or ideological seduction. It is important to appreciate the minimal and modest freedoms that enable a person largely to negotiate hindrances or live with unavoidable impediments. From the freedom of thought extoled in old folk songs, to the freedom of choice in simple life situations—coffee or tea?—that is so often dismissed by philosophy and theology, to the serene acceptance of one's diminishing powers in old age—a wealth of personal freedoms stands at our disposal that merit our appreciative acknowledgment. These freedoms animate and foster an extremely valuable *sense* of freedom, awakening and nourishing, moreover—to use the words of the philosopher Peter Bieri—a sense of being the "initiator" of one's will and the "subject" of one's life.[8] As do all feelings, however, so also does this one occasionally vacillate, or

7. Arendt, *Thinking without a Banister*, 378.
8. Peter Bieri, *Das Handwerk der Freiheit: Über die Entdeckung des eigenen Willens* (Munich: Hanser, 2001), 73. Wolfgang Huber returns repeatedly to this topic in *Von der Freiheit: Perspektiven für eine solidarische Welt* (Munich: Beck, 2012). Rüdiger Bittner objects that

even deceive us, while nonetheless remaining an important indicator of experienced or at least anticipated freedom.

The lingering reference to such forms of freedom, however, must not distract us from situations in which people are genuinely denied broader freedoms to shape their own lives especially in social and political situations. The spirit of freedom that remains mindful of the spirit of justice can in fact facilitate what we might call fruitful unrest with respect to such abuses of power and denied freedoms, ultimately awakening claims and demands for the sort of concrete actions that Heinrich Bedford-Strohm calls processes of "communicative freedom."[9]

Such stimuli are crucial in preventing a rigorous commitment and struggle against all forms of open and concealed slavery from weakening or even from being abandoned out of resignation. Here Elisabeth Schüssler Fiorenza's clearly articulated warning against the perennially seductive activation of Aristotelian ethos remains as timely as ever. Even in allegedly milder contemporary forms, an ethos that "maintains socio-political differences of gender, ethnicity, and slavery as *natural and therefore unchangeable*" must be rigorously challenged.[10]

The strength of a minimalist understanding of freedom (the freedom from barriers that is to be shrewdly discerned

---

"this concept of freedom eventually encounters the problem of the satisfied slave." Bittner, *Bürger sein*, 20–21.

9. Heinrich Bedford-Strohm, *Gemeinschaft aus kommunikativer Freiheit: Sozialer Zusammenhalt in der modernen Gesellschaft. Ein theologischer Beitrag* (Gütersloh: Gütersloher Verlagshaus, 1999).

10. Elisabeth Schüssler Fiorenza, "Slave Wo/men and Freedom in the Pauline Tradition: Some Methodological Reflections," in Welker, *Quests for Freedom*, 46–71, esp. 67; see also Ron Soodalter, "A Blight on the Nation: Slavery in Today's America," in Welker, *Quests for Freedom*, 14–25.

and fostered)[11] resides in its resolve to remain coolly objective and to focus on quotidian individual human existence. Yet even such admittedly valuable concentration
on the more modest personal forms of freedom becomes
precarious whenever one associates them with any and all
actions, as does Bittner: For "everything we do actually
curtails (and expands) the freedom of those with whom
we live. We are constantly in one another's way and yet
also constantly steadying the ladder for one another."[12]
But does such a view not trivialize the concepts of barriers
and hindrances and demote freedom itself to the notion of
"cautiously making one's way"? How can such individual-
istic freedom of caution and self-protection, as important
as it may well be, be prevented from obscuring the sense
of freedom deriving from experiences of community and
of belonging and from broader moral-political freedoms?[13]
How can one prevent this concentration on immediate *personal* freedoms from obscuring or making light of the fact
that at the same time freedom is being subjected to massive
and egregious *political* subversion?

Rüdiger Bittner's explications also make it clear that
such sober concentration on minimalist elementary freedoms can certainly be accompanied by problematic assessments of political-moral freedom. For example, Bittner considers international freedom rankings to be highly
questionable: "In effect, such freedom rankings measure
. . . not the freedom enjoyed by people in various countries,
but rather the similarity their political systems exhibit with
our own, and primarily with that of the United States."[14]

11. Bittner, *Bürger sein*, 51 and passim.
12. Bittner, *Bürger sein*, 51.
13. See in this regard the contributions in part 4 (Freedom as
Ethos of Belonging) of Welker, *Quests for Freedom*, 251–335.
14. Bittner, *Bürger sein*, 46.

He also comes to a remarkably relativist assessment with respect to circumstances in the Federal Republic of Germany and the former German Democratic Republic prior to the fall of the Berlin Wall in 1989: "If I may remain for a moment with the east-west comparison . . . one cannot say how much free access to news media *not* controlled by the state counts over against the freedom of job security; how much religious freedom counts over against security from poverty in old age; or how much free labor unions count over against cheap theater tickets."[15]

Bittner finds "different countries offering differently supplied baskets of average freedoms" and seems to maintain that one's preference of one such "freedom-mix," as he calls them, over another is ultimately simply a matter of opinion and taste. He also warns against the kind of political self-transfiguration that normally accompanies the lofty apodictic assertion that "we live in a free country!" Germany, he maintains, can be called "free" only owing to the basic freedoms set forth in its constitution, through which the Federal Republic guarantees its citizens "freedom of religion, opinion, and vocation" among others, a guarantee that for the most part is reliable thanks to the institutions that function to support it.[16] But how are such politically and legally ensured freedoms acquired, monitored, and defended? Here, too, one must discern and assess the multiplicity of necessary powers of the multimodal spirit of freedom that were and continue to be at work.

15. Bittner, *Bürger sein*, 46.
16. Bittner, *Bürger sein*, 41–42. The fundamental rights mentioned in the constitution include freedom of person, opinion, faith, assembly and resistance, eligibility for public office, and voting. Individual and economic freedoms and rights include the right to property, trades, freedom of choice of one's occupation or profession and place of work, and commerce.

This more relaxed view of various "freedom baskets" offered in different countries, however, rather than offering a genuinely sustaining answer, is instead almost irresponsible given the present situation of the world. It goes without saying that Western democracies based on freedom should not escape criticism when they succumb to self-adulation. However, one cannot but be profoundly disturbed by the obvious decline of important political rights—the right to choose political leaders in free and fair elections; the restricting and dismantling of freedom of the press and public expressions of opinion; the restriction of judicial independence; and finally intrusions into free scientific and scholarly research—in what were previously more or less free democracies.[17]

International civil and media-based vigilance is urgently required, though also political, legal, and economic measures to combat the proliferation of such comprehensive barriers and hindrances to freedom. The growth of aggressive chauvinist and xenophobic sentiment similarly diminishes freedom not only among those whom that sentiment excludes and subjects to hatred but also among those perpetrating and spreading such sentiment. The engagement of political, legal, educational, civil, media-based, and religious entities is urgently needed to counter such developments.

Societies such as the former German Democratic Republic, which carried on surveillance of its sixteen to seventeen million citizens by means of the so-called State Secret Service, or Stasi, with its more than 90,000 official

17. Michael J. Abramowitz, "Freedom in the World 2018: Democracy in Crisis," in Freedom House, *Freedom in the World 2018: The Annual Survey of Political Rights and Civil Liberties* (New York: Rowman, 2019), 1–9.

employees and 100,000–200,000 largely extorted "unofficial colleagues," and through actions that included spying, intimidation, harassment, and persecution; a country that prevented its citizens from leaving by erecting a wall staffed by deadly snipers; and that wholly undermined religious freedom and freedom of any public expression of opinion and assembly—such societies cannot be called free, despite full employment and cheap theater tickets.

The multimodal spirit of freedom makes it possible to appreciate what we have called the more modest personal freedoms without losing sight of formative moral and political freedoms as well as the inherent dangers that arise when freedom in society at large is undermined. Here an assessment of the complex inner constitution of pluralist societies and a sober understanding of the absolute necessity of moral communication can help us discern, articulate, and ultimately be inspired by the activities of the spirit of freedom.

Social Pluralism and the Fragility of Moral Freedom

On the one hand, free pluralist Western societies overtly affirm an understanding of individualism that is both colorful and varied. They acknowledge the human individual not only as a subject gifted with reason and will in the sense of Kant and other Enlightenment thinkers but also as a radically unique emotional-physical individual in the sense of Schleiermacher and many representatives of postmodern anthropology.[18] They claim, moreover, to

18. Cf. the nuanced view of Reinhold Niebuhr on "individuality in modern culture," in *Human Nature*, vol. 1 of *The Nature and Destiny of Man* (New York: Scribner, 1964), 54–92; and the complex

hold fast to the idea of human dignity, an idea that "contains probably the most radical principle of freedom and equality in history. Because that principle was introduced into a society that distinguished between master and slave, it demanded a fundamental paradigm change in legal and political thinking. Humanism associated this Christian idea with the beginnings of Greek and Roman jurisprudence in antiquity and enhanced it with an educational commission that urges human beings to evolve and develop their dignity both culturally and intellectually, though it makes no provisions for conditions guaranteeing that dignity."[19]

Former German constitutional judge Paul Kirchhof has referred to the idea of human dignity as a factor contributing to "ethical uneasiness in the law": "The constitutional guarantee of human dignity first of all provides a guiding principle for the entirety of the legal system, then also a fundamental legal principle enforceable through constitutional complaint in any given individual case. If the guarantee of inviolable human dignity asserts itself within a multiplicity of such individual cases, then this grand idea becomes a part of state praxis that benefits the individual."[20]

But affirmation of radical human individuality and at the same time radical affirmation of human freedom and

---

endeavors in "the creation of the sovereign self" described by Jean Bethke Elshtain, *Sovereignty: God, State, and Self* (New York: Basic Books, 2008), 159–80.

19. Paul Kirchhof, "Einführung in die Tagung," in *Die Menschenwürde als Verfassungsgrundlage,* ed. Burkhard Kämper and Klaus Pfeffer, *Essener Gespräche zum Thema Staat und Kirche*, vol. 51 (Münster: Aschendorf, 2019), 1. Cf. William Schweiker, "Presenting Theological Humanism," in *Theological Ethics and Global Dynamics: In the Time of Many Worlds* (Oxford: Blackwell, 2004), 199–219.

20. Kirchhof, "Einführung," 3–4.

equality—are these not utterly untenable utopias? Many people both outside and even inside late-modern pluralist societies find unrealistic or even illusory not only these fundamental affirmations of individuality coupled with simultaneous freedom and equality but also the expectation that such assumptions genuinely will be legally and politically implemented. They believe that should this assessment of free individuality and moral commitment to freedom and equality ever be genuinely implemented in praxis, the risk would involve nothing less than the utter relativism of worldviews accompanied by social chaos.

In reality, however, one can indeed observe the implementation and elaboration of such freedom in late-modern pluralist societies and in their channels of moral communication, notwithstanding the constant dangers to which they are subject. But what is it that morality really accomplishes? People in complex social relationships cannot live without morality. Through moral training and communication, people mutually judge the various aspects of their behavior. One thing is good, another bad. And they associate doing good with praise and doing bad with reproach. Expressed more broadly, we accord some behavior approval and respect while denying such to other behavior. Or we try to thwart such behavior by threatening such denial beforehand.

Viewed formally and minimalistically, moral communication consists precisely in this network of according or denying respect—that is, of the promise of respect and the threat of its denial.[21] Such accordance or denial can be expressed with varying degrees of vehemence. We can coolly

---

21. See Niklas Luhmann's thorough discussion, "Soziologie der Moral," in *Theorietechnik und Moral*, ed. Niklas Luhmann and Stephan H. Pfürtner (Frankfurt: Suhrkamp, 1978), esp. 43–63.

acknowledge that members of our family, our friends, or our colleagues are friendly and reliable and keep their promises and appointments. Such behavior constitutes the minimal expectation with respect to moral content. But we can also be delightfully surprised at the behavior and actions of others. In that case, respect in the sense of acknowledgment or observation turns into joy, admiration, and esteem. But we can also be deceived and disappointed. Such experiences can generate caution, mistrust, and bitterness. The worst cases, however, can cause enduring moral conflicts. Instead of simply diverging, our opinions and convictions enduringly collide. The indispensable element of mutual assessment and conclusions turns into harsh, often malevolent judgment and condemnation. In such cases, moral communication is clearly derailed.

The indispensability of moral communication prompts many people to believe somewhat naively that morality as such is invariably and always good. But that is a grievous misunderstanding. We need adduce not only the obvious examples of criminal morality or mafia morality but also examples of horrific political and religious moral corruption within larger demographic groups (such as fascism, apartheid, and ecological brutalism). Such distortion and poisoning of moral communication are not only quite conceivable but already constantly at work. Critics of social pluralism and its multicolored individualism see it constantly and helplessly exposed to such moral relativity. And yet individualism and free moral communication represent only one side of pluralist societies.

Pluralist societies are also formatively influenced by a limited plurality of organizations and institutions—what are known as social systems—that in their own turn explicitly are *not* shaped into a single monohierarchical form. Independent social systems deserving particular mention include politics, law, the media, the marketplace, science and scholarship, education, family, religion, health care, and defense systems. These are systems essential for all of society;[22] they provide a limited plurality of organized, institutionalized, and highly normative entities[23] with which individuals (with or without professional ties), individual moral representatives, and representatives of public morals at large within what are known as civil groups and associations must deal. Because these social systems are indeed aware that they are indispensable for the broader social community to flourish, they are keen on defending their internal structures in each and every one of their operations.[24] The division and balance of power that such entities develop within affirmed pluralist societies function in a

---

22. Cf. Welker, *Kirche im Pluralismus*, 13–24; Michael Welker, "Was ist Pluralismus?," in *Wertepluralismus*, Studium Generale der Universität Heidelberg 1998/99, ed. Christopher Balme (Heidelberg: C. Winter, 1999), 9–23.

23. The basic landscape of this complex of essential institutions and organizations is the focus of a series of international and interdisciplinary research projects whose results will be published beginning in 2020 by Evangelische Verlagsanstalt in Leipzig. The first four of ten volumes include Jürgen von Hagen et al., eds., *The Impact of the Market on Character Formation, Ethical Education, and the Communication of Values in Late Modern Pluralistic Societies*; Michael Welker et al., eds., *The Impact of Religion on Character Formation*; John Witte Jr. et al., eds., *The Impact of the Law on Character Formation*; William Schweiker et al., eds., *The Impact of Academic Research on Character Formation*.

24. Initial insights were provided in the excellent works by Talcott Parsons, *The Social System* (New York: Free Press, 1951); Talcott Parsons, *Sociological Theory and Modern Society* (New York: Free Press, 1967); Niklas Luhmann, *Soziale Systeme: Grundriss einer allgemeinen Theorie* (Frankfurt: Suhrkamp, 1984); Niklas Luhmann, *Die Gesellschaft der Gesellschaft* (Frankfurt: Suhrkamp, 1997).

multipolar and multimodal fashion to stimulate and foster freedom at various levels.

This more or less successful system of mutual correctives between social systems and their ongoing dealings with the moral engagements of individuals and their civil alliances within society is accompanied by a high degree of social freedom whose value simply cannot be overestimated. This impressive and ambitious cycle of power within pluralist societies represents a sublime but unfortunately highly endangered possession, something immediately evident not only in perennial attempts on the international stage by political, religious, or military powers to stem public activities within civil society and to subject the other social systems to their own hierarchical control. It is in a more creeping fashion that forces set in motion by the marketplace, the media, and technology are able to distort the balances of power in pluralist societies.

One obvious subversive power in this sense is the "accumulation of indoctrinated masses that are seduced by populist leaders,"[25] which many populists welcome and which, as seen in my first lecture, is ultimately responsible for the miseries of totalitarianism. Hannah Arendt also quite accurately discerned the dangers of a potential erosion of civil powers and institutions through epidemic egoism, conformism fostered by both politics and the media, and an enduring weakening of the influence of the family and education.[26] And finally, it is not least the deforming intrusions into civil organizations by the social systems that constitute a subversive threat. Jürgen Habermas issued a trenchant warning against these—as he put it—"system-

25. Habermas, *Between Facts and Norms*, 382.
26. Arendt, *The Human Condition*, 38–40.

paternalistic intrusions."[27] He draws attention not only to the imminent danger of a "supervisory state" but also to the destructive relationships between the electronic mass media and civil powers. Mass media manage, as Habermas puts it, to impose their power structures on the public sphere by a careful selection of topics, the repression of other topics, and the creation of illusory participation. He remarks, "The sociology of mass communications conveys a skeptical impression of the power-ridden, mass-media-dominated public spheres of Western democracies. Social movements, citizen initiatives and forums, political and other associations, in short, the groupings of civil society, are indeed sensitive to problems, but the signals they send out and the impulses they give are generally too weak to initiate learning processes or redirect decision making in the political system in the short run."[28] His extremely pessimistic assessment is that "such associations certainly do not represent the most conspicuous element of a public sphere dominated by mass media and large agencies, observed by market and opinion research, and inundated by the public relations work, propaganda, and advertising of political parties and groups."[29]

27. Habermas, *Between Facts and Norms*, 351–52 and passim.

28. Habermas, *Between Facts and Norms*, 373; see in this regard Günter Thomas and Michael Welker, "Einleitung: Religiöse Funktionen des Fernsehens?," in *Religiöse Funktionen des Fernsehens? Medien-, kultur- und religionswissenschaftliche Perspektiven*, ed. Günter Thomas (Opladen: Westdeutscher Verlag, 2000), 9–25.

29. Habermas, *Between Facts and Norms*, 367; cf. also the pessimistic views of Niklas Luhmann, *Soziologie des Risikos* (Berlin: de Gruyter 1999); and *Ökologische Kommunikation: Kann die moderne Gesellschaft sich auf ökologische Gefährdungen einstellen?* (Opladen: Westdeutscher Verlag, 1986). See also the risky ponderings by Michael Ignatieff, *The Lesser Evil: Political Ethics in an Age of Terror* (Edinburgh: Edinburgh University Press, 2005).

Habermas believes that processes of moral communication simply are not up to the task of providing the necessary formative impulses, for their efforts to demand that social systems promote justice and freedom are variously weakened. But what role does religion now play in this extraordinarily complex description of the power cycle within free pluralist societies?

The Power of Religion—but of What Sort?

The multimodal spirit of justice, freedom, truth, and peace is no chimera despite its being ignored, distorted, and dismissed. For religious persons, and certainly for those seized by it, it represents a divine gift that not only shapes them in many ways but also equips them with many gifts and powers. At the end of the previous lecture, I drew attention especially to the religious emphasis on the enormous breadth of human existence, to the capacity of religious thinking to encompass broad temporal horizons, and in that context also to the religious potential for strengthening the multimodal activity of the spirit on behalf of justice and protection of the weak. I must unfortunately dash any expectation that at the end of this present lecture I might proceed similarly by emphasizing the institutional and moral power of religion as a guarantee of unconditionally good morality and as an impetus for promoting the spirit of freedom. For proceeding thus would almost constitute gross negligence. Allow me to explain.

One must not, of course, underestimate the enormous institutional power of religion despite the plethora of announcements of its demise and decline in today's world. Its considerable potential for serving as a source of power for healthy morality and for freedom, however, is by no means guaranteed simply by virtue of its institutional status. Slightly varying statistics suggest that 84 percent of the world's inhabitants currently belong—with varying degrees of engagement—to a religious community, a number that statistics also predict might even increase to 87 percent over the next few decades.[30] The question frequently raised twenty years ago, and not just by politicians—namely, whether humankind would be moving into the future *with* or *without* religion—has shifted slightly to the question whether we will be moving into the future with *cultivated* or *uncultivated* (meaning tyrannical or chaotic) religiosity.

Almost a third of the world's present population currently professes Christianity (2.26 billion, numerically ahead of 1.57 billion Muslims and 900 million Hindus). Approximately 72 percent of Europeans profess Christianity today. However, these current numbers are shifting now especially to the detriment of Christians and Europeans. Given current trends, in fifty years it will be not only Muslims but also followers of other religions who have overtaken Christians in numbers. One must consider too the steady growth of agnostics and atheists, who at least in Europe currently constitute 23 percent of the population.

Given these statistics, one can quite legitimately emphasize the need not only for enhanced ecumenical dialogue between the various Christian denominations and increasing interreligious dialogue but also increased dialogue concerning broader issues of worldview with those with no denominational affiliation, with agnostics or athe-

30. Gustav Theile, "Das neue Jahrhundert der Religionen," *Frankfurter Allgemeine Zeitung*, October 27, 2019; for a more detailed view of global religious developments see Detlef Pollack and Gergely Rosta, *Religion in der Moderne: Ein internationaler Vergleich* (Frankfurt/New York: Campus Verlag, 2015).

ists critical of religion, and with those who for various reasons are indifferent to questions of worldview. What is most necessary, however, is a self-critical and informative examination of the creeping processes of alienation and secularization *within* religions themselves, in which context the disrupted relationship many religions have with the spirit of freedom cannot but play an especially crucial role. For although essentially all religions eagerly engage politically and legally granted freedoms in furthering their own activities and proselytizing, do those same religions also promote the spirit of freedom through a willingness to remain critically and self-critically attentive to their own lapses, including in promoting equitable and just life circumstances in society?

In 2014 the *Journal of Law and Religion* published the findings of the symposium "Re-Thinking Religious Freedom," which derived from a series of studies within the project "Politics of Religious Freedom: Contested Norms and Local Practices (PRF)" sponsored by the Henry R. Luce Initiative on Religion and International Affairs beginning in 2010 with consultations in Europe, the Near East (or Middle East), Southern Asia, and the United States of America. These studies focused on interrelations between institutionalized politics, law, and religious politics, and the effects these relations exert on religious communities. Conflicts between and even within these same communities also provided topics of discussion. But the findings were quite sobering, with numerous contributions demonstrating "how the politics of religious freedom has been shaped by a majoritarian politics to serve its own ends."[31]

31. Elizabeth Shakman Hurd and Winnifred Fallers Sullivan, "Symposium: Re-Thinking Religious Freedom, Editors' Introduction," *Journal of Law and Religion* 29 (2014): 358.

In a word, the topic of "freedom" had essentially become the topic of self-preservation and self-enhancement. Although individual developments promoting the freedom of religious minorities were assessed, there was also ample evidence of power or turf struggles between these same minorities, including the development of political strategies to repress or displace internal differences.[32] This overt politicization of the struggle for religious freedom, driven not only by politics but certainly also by religious leadership itself, presents us with a grim, almost belligerent tableau.

These discouraging findings with respect to political and religious leadership and its unwillingness to step forth on behalf of justice and freedom is confirmed by studies of the relationship between Christianity and human rights. In the introduction to his book with that very title—namely, *Christianity and Human Rights*—John Witte Jr. remarks laconically: "Likewise, some of the nations given to the most belligerent forms of religious oppression have ratified more of the international human rights instruments than the United States has, and have crafted more elaborate bills of rights than what appears in the United States Constitution."[33]

It is not just bigoted political attitudes but also repulsive and unseemly struggles within religious communities themselves that disclose a profoundly disturbed relationship between those same communities and the commitment to freedom. Witte demonstrates with unequivocal clarity how many evangelical groups within Western churches and societies associate the very notion of demo-

32. Cf. Hurd and Sullivan, "Re-Thinking Religious Freedom."

33. John Witte Jr., "Introduction," in *Christianity and Human Rights: An Introduction*, ed. John Witte Jr. and Frank S. Alexander (Cambridge: Cambridge University Press, 2010), 11.

cratic freedom with materialism and egoistic individualism and also dismiss the very concept of pluralism in a blanket fashion as being wholly negative. They similarly view free forms of religious speech as well as freedom of the press and freedom of assembly with resolute skepticism.

In another example, Witte reveals that a deep chasm separates the declaration of the Twenty-Fifth Clergy-Laity Congress of the Greek Orthodox Archdiocese of North and South America (1980) that affirms numerous basic church rights,[34] on the one hand, and observable current praxis in other parts of Orthodox churches, on the other. He remarks with some restraint that "today the Orthodox Church's commitment to human rights and democratic principles is being tested more severely than ever before— particularly in Russia and Eastern Europe."[35]

Over against the prevalent tendency to engage in religious, political, and moral self-righteousness, he maintains, "It is undeniable that religion has been, and still is, a formidable force for both political good and political evil, that it has fostered both benevolence and belligerence, peace and pathos of untold dimensions. But the proper response to religious belligerence and pathos cannot be to deny that religion exists or to dismiss it to the private sphere and sanctuary. The proper response is to castigate the vices and to cultivate the virtues of religion."[36]

It is important not to lose sight of the acute ambivalence attaching to the institutional and even moral power of religion. At the same time, however, the undeniable and overwhelming *institutional* power of religion must not

---

34. Stanley Harakas, "Human Rights: An Eastern Orthodox Perspective," *Journal of Ecumenical Studies* 19 (1982): 13, 21, 26.

35. Witte, *Christianity and Human Rights*, 35.

36. Witte, *Christianity and Human Rights*, 41–42.

precipitately be mistaken for religious *freedom*. Such also applies to the path and perspectives of what is known as natural theology, which disregards the specific form and content of religious communities. Precisely within the framework of an anthropologically and ethically engaged natural theology, one can quickly acknowledge that the beneficent power and radiant influence bestowed on religions ultimately derives precisely from the spirit of justice, freedom, truth, and peace that is also bestowed on them. Indeed, it is only to the extent that religions are seized and shaped by this very spirit and then allow these bequeathed powers and spiritual gifts to assert themselves in a self-critical fashion that the spirit of freedom can become active within and venture forth from them.

Conclusion

The multimodal spirit of freedom should be acknowledged even in its elementary forms. In that context, Rüdiger Bittner's suggestion that one understand freedom as freedom from barriers throws into relief those particular efforts in which everyone engages in daily life to avoid more effectively both actual and potential barriers. Bittner similarly draws attention to the dangers inhering within the comprehensive but sometimes illusory feelings and envisioned agenda of freedom. The resulting increased awareness of the multifaceted nature of these practical freedoms we exercise in daily life should not lose sight, however, of the relationship between the spirit of freedom and the spirit of justice.

This challenge requires that one seek political and moral means of shaping the agenda of freedom within society—including at the level of civil society—in order to better deal with the more compact forms of social

subversions of freedom. Here the limited but also potentially illusory possibilities of freedom within pluralist societies and their channels of moral communication play
a significant role.

With respect to religion, one must critically and especially self-critically examine the dangerous confusion
between freedom, on the one hand, and institutional
power and power aggrandizement, on the other. Taking
one's orientation from the multimodal spirit of freedom,
justice, truth, and peace facilitates the articulation of a
natural-theological realism and an exemplary ethos of the
sort addressed in the second lecture in connection with
the post-1980 movement of renewal in Poland and parts
of Eastern Europe.

CALLED TO TRUTH

How do we understand the multimodal spirit of truth, the activities of which extend from the familiar notion of accuracy or correctness to a worldwide network of research and teaching among university scientists and scholars with all the operations attaching to the search for truth and the testing of resulting truth claims? Truth claims are measured and tested against standards of accuracy, certainty, consensus, coherence, and so on. At the same time, organized, methodologically rigorous, innovative research is initiated with the goal of disclosing and acquiring new knowledge commensurate with these standards.

After these general considerations in part 1, part 2 of this lecture describes such a search for truth as conducted by a group of international and interdisciplinary scientists and scholars seeking to expand their approaches to anthropology and whose findings can acquire relevance for an anthropology shaped from the perspective of natural theology.

Part 3 then describes concepts of God within natural theology that might support such anthropological findings. What emerges is that claims to universal validity asserted by theological doctrines of God not tied to specific religious traditions prove untenable and, further, that the insights and assertions of natural theology itself must be subjected to modern critiques of religion. Part 3 also opens a discussion of whether the assertion from the theology of revelation that "God is spirit and seeks to be worshiped in spirit and truth" can be rendered as an assertion commensurate with natural theology.

Viewed in a general and formal sense, the spirit, as the young Hegel put it, is an active power that generates and influences relationships through combination and differentiation. Attempts to deal meaningfully with this complex power have tended to concentrate on the spirit's manifestations in bipolar constellations—for example, in subject and object; cognition and object of cognition; I and Thou; person and fellow person; self and other; self and world; God and human being. Such bipolar constellations have served to facilitate an access to truth in which truth is understood as the coincidence of thinking and its object or of subjective assertions and facts of the objective world, or similar relationships.[1] The following discussion will assess bipolar constellations as manifestations of the multimodal spirit while simultaneously objecting when such manifestations are taken as absolute.

Truth within the Arc Extending from Accuracy to Internationally Organized Scientific and Scholarly Searches for Truth

As earlier in the lecture on freedom, allow me here, too, to commence with an elementary definition. The most rudimentary understanding of truth is simple accuracy, which is applicable to both judgments and actions. Is something just as it was conceived or asserted and as it was observed?

1. See, e.g., Thomas Aquinas, *Summa theologiae*, I, q. 16, a. 2: "veritas est adaequatio rei et intellectus."

Is the statement concerning it correct? Did a particular act genuinely proceed thus and not otherwise? Viewing something as accurate provides at least a preliminary element of security both in judgment and in one's confidence of being able to provide knowledge capable of rational and intersubjective substantiation.

The self-evident nature of our dealings with such assumptions of correctness in daily life, though also their occasionally swift collapse, should not mislead us into downplaying this elementary mode of multimodal truth and its ascertainment. To take but one example: "Michael Welker in Nehren outside Tübingen can be reached by telephone at 074736620." This information was correct and the statement thus true in the years prior to August 1987. Its accuracy and veracity could be ascertained by a glance at the telephone book, by inquiries among Michael Welker's acquaintances, and of course by dialing the number itself. Today, however, this statement is true only with qualification—that is, "Michael Welker *could be* reached in Nehren outside Tübingen by telephone until mid-1987 under the number 074736620." That the statement *was* correct is irrelevant today, and its truth, as Hegel so eloquently expressed it, has become "stale."[2]

Citing a dramatic dispute concerning truth—namely, the famous case of Galileo—Alfred North Whitehead underscored how important it is to qualify statements that make truth claims:

Galileo said that the earth moves and that the sun is fixed; the Inquisition said that the earth is fixed and the

2. Thus Hegel's comment on attempts to fix the impression of sensory certainty as truth by writing it down. Hegel, *Phenomenology of Spirit*, 62.

sun moves; and Newtonian astronomers, adopting an absolute theory of space, said that both the sun and the earth move. But now we say that any one of these three statements is equally true, provided that you have fixed your sense of "rest" and "motion" in a way required by the statement adopted. At the date of Galileo's controversy with the Inquisition, Galileo's way of stating the facts was, beyond question, the fruitful procedure for the sake of scientific research. But in itself it was not more true than the formulation of the Inquisition. But at that time the modern concepts of relative motion were in nobody's mind; so that the statements were made in ignorance of the qualifications required for their more perfect truth. Yet this question of the motions of the earth and the sun expresses a real fact in the universe; and all sides had got hold of important truths concerning it. But with the knowledge of those times, the truths appeared to be inconsistent.[3]

The Inquisition supported the perspective of healthy human understanding, to which the German children's mnemonic rhyme still applies even today:

> The sun rises in the East,
> turns south at midday's feast;
> in the North it's never seen,
> in the West it sets serene.

That is, it supported the perspective of sensory certainty with its powerful truth claim. After all, "anyone can see

---

3. Alfred North Whitehead, *Science and the Modern World* (Cambridge: Cambridge University Press, 1953; paperback ed. 2011), 227–28.

that the sun rises in the East!" From the modern perspective, of course, a certain element of irony attaches to the
fact that it was these same inquisitors as representatives of
the Christian religion who, with their own truth claims—
for example, faith in the resurrection—first presented
enormous challenges to healthy human understanding
and sensory certainty and yet then appealed to this *same*
healthy human understanding and sensory certainty to
counter new scientific findings of astronomy. As is well
known, the church has still not entirely recovered from
the loss of trust it incurred with that earlier decision.

The case of Galileo throws considerable light on the
limited capacity of (sensory) certainty in the search and
defense of truth. For one cannot assert that "truth is accessible to human beings solely in the mode of *certitude*;
... [one cannot assert that] truth is accessible to us only to
the extent we are fully aware and convinced of the truth.
At the same time, such certitude can exhibit widely varying gradations and be accompanied, challenged, and called
into question to varying degrees by doubt."[4] Despite this
important restriction, such *"certitudinal* orientation," or
the linking of truth to certainty, remains problematic,[5] for
a great many acts performed within our conscious lives are
sustained by knowledge of truth quite without the more
or less explicit elimination of irritation and doubt that allegedly characterizes our sense of certainty.[6]

4. Wilfried Härle, "Das christliche Verständnis der Wahrheit," in
Wahrheit, Marburger Jahrbuch Theologie, vol. 21, ed. Wilfried Härle
and Rainer Breuel (Leipzig: EVA, 2009), 82.

5. Thus Julian Nida-Rümelin, *Demokratie und Wahrheit* (Munich:
Beck, 2006), 45, accompanied by the warning that "certitudinalism
promotes intolerance" (46).

6. Cf. Ludwig Wittgenstein's reflections and meditations on the
complex weave of presuppositions and conditions that necessarily

Human beings constantly live with trust not only in innumerable assumptions of accuracy but also in numerous
assumptions of accuracy supported by proven truth claims
about which *they themselves* have in fact *not* personally established certainty. The extent to which such truth claims
must be proven, of course, can vary widely, a situation in
its own turn leading to disputes concerning their tenability. Such also applies to the *consensus theory of truth* based
on the coordination of a multiplicity of certainties, and to
the *coherence theory of truth*, which views the compatible
interrelation of knowledge and assertions to be a necessary
condition for making truth claims.

It is important to realize that no personal truth search,
though also no scientifically supported truth search, is
in a position "to claim that it achieves absolute certainty
beyond the possibility of any further refinement or cor-
rection. Rather, its achievement will be gaining a degree
of understanding which is sufficiently insightful in its ex-
planatory character for its acceptance to be something to
which it is entirely rational to commit oneself."[7] In numerous dialogues between theology and the natural sciences,
John Polkinghorne and I have posed the question of what
exactly characterizes "truth-seeking associations" in science and religion. We have found that, on the one hand,
the search for truth seeks to solidify and stabilize certainties and to attain concurrence and as broad a consensus as
possible concerning those certainties. On the other hand,
the search for truth seeks to attain and then expand the
element of coherent understanding. Although these two

accompany the notion of "certainty," in *Über Gewissheit*, vol. 8 of
Werkausgabe (Frankfurt: Suhrkamp, 1984), esp. 140–42.

7. John Polkinghorne, "The Search for Truth," in *The Science and
Religion Dialogue: Past and Future*, ed. Michael Welker (Frankfurt:
Lang, 2014), 53.

operations—one focusing on consensus, the other on coherence—often enough variously irritate each other, that same irritation contributes toward making the search for truth a productive process.[8]

The formally organized search for truth does enjoy several advantages, for example, by offering an enormous inventory of tested and refuted truth claims and thus providing elements of truth that at least for the moment are verifiable. The inherent mutual correctives obtaining between specialists in a given field along with the presence of severe sanctions—for example, damage to one's reputation as a result of certifying untenable truth claims—enable organized science and scholarship to offer an important defense system against error and deception in the various disciplines. And by virtue of its status as a training center for those interested in moving into responsible positions of leadership in society, it also is able to dispatch or mediate, as it were, its own ethos of truth and multimodal spirit of truth to all spheres of life. Its "heart" is found in the universities that throughout the world combine research and teaching and through the granting of doctoral degrees train qualified individuals for conducting future research.[9]

Accuracy, certainty, consensus, coherence, commensurability, tested and proven knowledge claims—these are

8. John Polkinghorne and Michael Welker, *Faith in the Living God: A Dialogue* (London: SPCK, 2001; 2nd ed., Eugene, OR: Cascade, 2019), chap. 9.

9. Thus the characterization offered by the jurist Joachim Lege in "Die Herzkammer der Wissenschaft: Das Wissenschaftssystem braucht ein Zentrum, das bahnbrechende Erfindungen mit dem wissenschaftlichen und gesellschaftlichen Konsens vermittelt. Das können nur die Universitäten sein," *Frankfurter Allgemeine Zeitung* (September 19, 2019): N4.

some of the criteria used in evaluating truth claims within the context of any search for truth.

Yet the spirit of truth that tests, evaluates, and ultimately confirms truth claims is but a single, albeit important, part of the organized system of science and scholarship. The ongoing stimulating pedagogical exchange with new generations of students and the enthusiasm and competition within research operations themselves are sustained by the commitment to the search for truth for the sake of creative, expanded knowledge. The fact that attention is occasionally and quite justifiably drawn to pioneering innovations outside organized research institutions militates not at all against the sustaining value of an organized system of research, scholarship, and teaching.[10]

An element of ethical significance is also attributed to the spirit of truth that radiates far beyond the sphere of science and scholarship out into society at large. The Berlin philosopher Volker Gerhardt considers it a "danger to Western civilization" that the current president of the United States of America consistently disregards truth in an effort to cultivate his own image, claiming to do so, moreover, for the sake of doing what is allegedly economically

10. Jochen Taupitz, "Das hohe Gut der Wissenschaftsfreiheit: Forschung zwischen Erkenntnisgewinn und Risikoproblem," *Forschung und Lehre* 26 (2019): 446. The self-imposed system of mutual checks and balances is one of the essential characteristics of science and scholarship. Science and scholarship constitute an autonomously corrected system committed to the attainment of knowledge that includes the entirety of the previously acknowledged and accepted findings of humankind that have been critically tested and indeed are perpetually accessible to critical testing. Research as the fundamental methodology of science and scholarship is thus committed to the goal of attaining secured knowledge of the objects of its examinations through methodical and systematic study that in its own turn is similarly accessible to testing.

best for his country. Massive amounts of incorrect information and assertions are sent out into the world in the guise
of "truths."[11] Gerhardt also observes, however, that

> as desperate as the situation indeed is, this presiden-
> tial renunciation of truth has accomplished one good
> thing, namely, bring to an end within a few weeks the
> dismissal of truth that for much too long had already
> been viewed as unsurpassably modern (or even as al-
> ready "postmodern"). Whereas until the spring of that
> year [2017] attributing *any* meaning at all to "truth"
> was considered a sign of unequivocal backwardness,
> there is now a rush to remove any and all doubt about
> the indispensability of truth not only in "marches for
> science," but also in academic circles.[12]

Gerhardt justifiably insists that people had "underesti-
mated the moral significance of truth while overestimating
its metaphysical status." When the will to assert serious and
resilient truth claims is abandoned, we lose our moorings
in thinking, acting, and interacting. It is precisely the "relativity of the human experience of world" and the "variety,
contrariness, and even enduring irreconcilability of positions that must make us conscious that, indeed, nothing

11. On April 29, 2019, the *Washington Post* published 10,000 false
assertions that had been disseminated by Donald Trump since he
took office in January 2017.

12. Volker Gerhardt, "In Vergessenheit geraten: Über die Unverzichtbarkeit der Wahrheit," *Forschung und Lehre* 24 (2017): 755. Concerning the enormous destructive power of such a cynical attitude
toward truth and accuracy within the weave of politics, the media,
and the broader public sphere, see also Romy Jaster and David Lanius, *Die Wahrheit schafft sich ab: Wie Fake News Politik machen*, 2nd
ed. (Stuttgart: Reclam, 2019).

is more urgent now than to hold fast to truth."[13] During the past few years, an international and interdisciplinary research project dedicated to an expanded understanding of certain aspects of anthropology in this sense has yielded findings that are both promising for science and scholarship and revealing for the human ethos.

An Interdisciplinary Search for Truth and Its Discovery of a Differentiated Natural-Theological Anthropology

The dialogue project "Science and Religion" was initially strongly shaped by philosophically interested theologians, religious scholars, and physicists. In his 1989–1991 Gifford Lectures, Ian Barbour described four models applicable to this dialogue—namely, "conflict, independence, dialogue, integration."[14] Although these models were later refined and expanded,[15] the fundamentally bipolar constellation continued to assert itself even as the field of natural science expanded to include biology, neurology, and psychology, and that of theology and philosophy to include historical and exegetical disciplines. We spent several exhausting years struggling with the dual "physicalist-mentalist approach" and with the question of whether the two areas might be amalgamated into a single theoretical framework. One particularly well-received reaction to the question "Monist or dualist approach?" was "We need a

13. Gerhardt, "In Vergessenheit geraten," 756.
14. Ian Barbour, *Religion in an Age of Science: The Gifford Lectures, 1989–1991*, vol. 1 (San Francisco: Harper, 1990), 4–30.
15. See, e.g., Niels Henrik Gregersen and Wentzel Van Huyssteen, *Rethinking Theology and Science: Six Models for the Current Dialogue* (Grand Rapids: Eerdmans, 1998).

dual-aspect monism."[16] After several years of consultations and assessment of the broad spectrum of truth claims coming from the various scientific and scholarly disciplines, we concluded programmatically that—at least in our shared work in the field of anthropology—we needed a "multidimensional approach."[17]

I myself initiated an international consultation extending over several years with colleagues from physics, biology, psychology, philosophy, religious studies, and systematic, ethical, historical, and biblical theology. The commitment to a multidimensional approach came to expression in the title "Body, Soul, Spirit: The Complexity of the Human Person." I confess that the first meeting began with a severe shock for me as the organizer, for the analytical philosopher Andreas Kemmerling quickly issued the following noteworthy warning: "Although you are intent on scrutinizing and possibly overcoming dualistic approaches to anthropology, nonetheless by concentrating on the 'complexity of the human person' you will fall into a bottomless pit." Kemmerling proceeded to explicate his fundamental skepticism over against precisely

16. Cf. Warren Brown, Nancey Murphy, and H. Newton Malony, eds., *Whatever Happened to the Soul? Scientific and Theological Portraits of Human Nature* (Philadelphia: Fortress, 1998).

17. Cf. Niels H. Gregersen, Willem B. Drees, and Ulf Görman, eds., *The Human Person in Science and Theology* (Edinburgh: T&T Clark, 2000); John Polkinghorne, ed., *The Work of Love: Creation as Kenosis* (Grand Rapids: Eerdmans; London: SPCK, 2001); Malcolm Jeeves, ed., *From Cells to Souls—and Beyond: Changing Portraits of Human Nature* (Grand Rapids: Eerdmans, 2004); R. Kendall Soulen and Linda Woodhead, eds., *God and Human Dignity* (Grand Rapids: Eerdmans, 2006); Michael Welker, "Relation: Human and Divine," in *The Trinity and an Entangled World: Relationality in Physical Science and Theology*, ed. J. Polkinghorne (Grand Rapids: Eerdmans, 2010), 157-67.

this approach. Philosophy and its neighboring disciplines, he explained, engage over twenty concepts of person that resist any clear organizing principle. How do you intend to impose order and clarity on these concepts? A person, for example, "is an individual capable of rationality; is responsible for what it does; has dignity; is not a something . . . but a someone . . . ; is free; is a unity of a body and a mind (soul); . . . is an intelligent agent, capable of . . . happiness, and misery; is an end in itself and an object of respect; is an entity to which both mental and physical properties can be ascribed; is capable of treating others as persons; is capable of verbal communication; is conscious and self-conscious."[18]

Amid this obvious derailment of our very point of departure, unanticipated succor came from the field of New Testament studies. Gerd Theissen delivered a lecture on Paul's understanding of the flesh and the body that both surprised and inspired many of us.[19] He demonstrated that Paul's anthropology cannot be fully grasped or comprehended on the basis of the offensive dualism of "flesh and spirit." Instead, what Paul is in fact offering is an ambitious anthropology with surprising syntheses and differentiations. The body, for example, cannot simply be identified with predatory flesh focused on self-preservation but is instead the locus of various energies associated with the soul and spirit, hence the locus of the polyphonous interaction between *all* its members and a source of multidimensional

18. Andreas Kemmerling, "Was macht den Begriff der Person so besonders schwierig?," in *Gegenwart des lebendigen Christus*, ed. Günter Thomas and Andreas Schüle (Leipzig: EVA, 2007), 545 (= "Why Is Personhood Conceptually Difficult?," in Welker, *Depth of the Human Person*, 25).

19. Theissen, "*Sarx, Soma,* and the Transformative *Pneuma*," in Welker, *Depth of the Human Person*.

psychosomatic resonance. The oft-lamented sharp dualism between flesh and spirit in fact marks what for Paul is the extremely important distinction between finitude (flesh) and eternity (spirit). The fleshly and spiritual body, moreover, though also the fleshly and spiritual heart (an organ of emotional, cognitive, and volitional energy), along with the psychosomatic unity of the soul emphasize various aspects of the differentiated totality of the human person. Paul's differentiation between reason and spirit and his non-bipolar understanding of conscience are also of considerable import here. The human conscience is not simply one's inner voice but rather an entire forum of voices that both accuse and defend, and that must first pass through other human faculties before arriving at a certain degree of concentration and inner peace.

Inspiringly gifted, Hellenistically trained, an educated Pharisee and citizen of Rome and indeed of the world, multicontextually oriented toward the needs of different church communities—Paul engages travel and epistolary correspondence as communication media and in so doing offers a multifaceted anthropology that makes it possible to illuminate interrelations between the varied cognitive powers and experiential spheres.[20] His approach also makes it possible to critique inculcated anthropological dualisms (body-soul, body-spirit) yet also brings to clearer expression anthropological entities such as soul and spirit that in many scholarly fields outside theology have long become obsolete. Although his anthropology is indeed tied

---

20. Michael Welker, "Die Anthropologie des Paulus als interdisziplinäre Kontakttheorie," in *Jahrbuch der Heidelberger Akademie der Wissenschaften für 2009*, ed. Heidelberg Akademie der Wissenschaften (Heidelberg: Universitätsverlag, Winter 2010), 98–108 (= "Flesh—Body—Heart—Soul—Spirit: Paul's Anthropology as an Interdisciplinary Bridge-Theory," in Welker, *Depth of the Human Person*, 45–57).

to a theology of revelation, its fundamental insights can also be clearly explicated and applied at the level of natural theology. These same insights provide considerable impetus and direction for disclosing a multimodal understanding of the human spirit and (as already seen in my second lecture) for providing a solid basis on which to critique the bipolar-intellectualistic conception.

Such an anthropological approach commensurate with natural theology can also be disclosed in other areas of the biblical tradition similarly located within contexts of a theology of revelation. The Tübingen Old Testament scholar Bernd Janowski recently published a comprehensive "anthropology of the Old Testament"[21] that takes its orientation from the various stages of human life and makes quite clear that the lives of people in ancient Israel were characterized by "experiences of corporeality, the ethos of justice, and a consciousness of finitude." Janowski discloses a whole array of phenomena involving human faculties and social relationships that was determinative not only for biblical Israel but also for vast stretches of the world of antiquity at large, and which is also quite capable of providing cognitive anthropological impulses for today's world. This particular mode of operation that focuses on a broad selection of culturally and religio-historically oriented disciplines and their claims to knowledge similarly provides a promising contribution to natural theology.

21. Bernd Janowski, *Anthropologie des Alten Testaments: Grundfragen—Kontexte—Themenfelder* (Tübingen: Mohr Siebeck, 2019).

"God as Spirit"—Translating a Statement from the Theology of Revelation into a Statement Commensurate with Natural Theology

The first example of the expression "natural theology" is found in Panaetius, the founder of Middle Stoicism. Panaetius used the term for the philosophical doctrine of God as distinct from the mythical theology of the poets on the one side, and on the other the political theology of the cults that the states set up and supported.[22]

Wolfhart Pannenberg quite rightly notes that the philosophical doctrine of God is to be designated as "natural" because it "corresponds to the nature of the divine itself, unfalsified by the political interests related to the state cults or by the literary imaginings, or lies, of the poets"[23]—a cogent enough explanation that does, however, beg the question of what exactly corresponds to the "nature [and truth] of the divine itself."

Because natural theology tries to speak about questions of religion and worldviews such that its statements are universally valid—a not insignificant challenge—theological and philosophical traditions have sought refuge in the conceptual world of speculative metaphysics when speaking about God. They have adduced "the Absolute," "the Infinite," "the Eternal," "the One and Undivided," "the Highest Being," and all sorts of "ultimate ideas" to render such references valid or acceptable to all religions and cultures. These lofty abstractions, moreover, have been

---

22. Wolfhart Pannenberg, *Systematic Theology*, vol. 3, trans. Geoffrey W. Bromiley (1994; London: T&T Clark, 2004), 76.
23. Pannenberg, *Systematic Theology*, 3:77.

generally accompanied by considerable and quite resolute truth claims.

Similar metaphysical references came to deft expression in a presentation given by a philosopher in the Heidelberg Academy of Science and Humanities under the title "God in Thinking: Why Philosophy Cannot Dispense with the Question of God."[24] To the astonishment of many academy members, however, who thought theology ought to welcome such accommodating responsiveness from philosophy, not every reaction was positive. A jurist, for example, wondered what such speculative notions of God had to do with divine justice and, indeed, whether notions of God that abstract from the admittedly difficult topic of God's justice were really referring to a God at all. A theologian similarly wondered whether metaphysical notions of God were not soteriologically empty—that is, whether they were not devoid of God's sustaining, saving, and elevating activities. Considerable doubts persisted concerning whether speculative ideas contributed anything toward enabling natural theology to speak at all, as it claims, about the essence and nature of God.

Tradition has been inclined to maneuver past the thorny problems created for theology by such "ultimate" metaphysical ideas concerning God by invoking a cosmogonic overlay, as it were, of the first, last, and highest being, to wit, by portraying God as the all-creating and "all-determinative primal force." But even this primitive form of understanding creation has become increasingly beset by questions and doubts, forced as it is to constantly ignore the

24. Jens Halfwassen, "Gott im Denken: Warum die Philosophie auf die Frage nach Gott nicht verzichten kann," in *Gott—Götter—Götzen: XIV. Europäischer Kongress für Theologie*, Veröffentlichungen der Wissenschaftlichen Gesellschaft für Theologie, vol. 38, ed. Christoph Schwöbel (Leipzig: EVA, 2013), 187–96.

varied ambivalence of nature and natural life and being unable to provide any persuasive response to the question of the efficaciousness of a just and beneficent God in a world so overtly replete with inequitably distributed suffering.

Critiques of religion both outside and inside theological circles have not surprisingly concentrated on this disastrous mix of speculative metaphysics and implausible cosmology.

The most incisive forms of such criticism were developed in Germany during the nineteenth-century period of early European modernity by Karl Marx and Friedrich Nietzsche, both of whom are still viewed as the classic authors of modern critiques of religion. These two thinkers engaged critically not only with the Christian religion itself and its understanding of piety but also with their own religio-critical and socio-critical philosophical predecessors. That is, they attacked not only illusory religious worldviews but also religio-critical, moralizing philosophies and, in Nietzsche's case, other fields in which scientific and moral truth claims were being made. This mode of operation enhanced the impact of their own critiques of religion, and because these critiques expanded into a more sweeping critique of worldviews and culture, they also possess relevance for natural theology that makes universal truth claims.

The most astute representatives of twentieth-century German-speaking Christian theology—here I will mention only Karl Barth, Dietrich Bonhoeffer, and Paul Tillich—took careful note of these broadly conceived critiques of religion, morality, and worldviews. They recognized that any Christian theology intent on avoiding not only religious and metaphysical illusions and wishful thinking but also political-moral ideologies can profit considerably from both Marx and Nietzsche.

The most trenchant remarks from Karl Marx in this regard are the following, where he speaks of

> man, who has found only the reflection of himself in the fantastic reality of heaven where he sought a supernatural being. . . . Religion is the self-consciousness and self-esteem of man who has either not yet found himself or has already lost himself again. But man is not an abstract being squatting outside the world. Man is the world of men, the state, society. This state and this society produce religion, which is an inverted consciousness of the world because they are an inverted world. . . . It is the fantastic realization of the human essence inasmuch as the human essence possesses no true reality. The struggle against religion is therefore indirectly the struggle against that world whose spiritual aroma is religion.[25]

That is, the struggle against religion is ultimately a struggle against the inverted or indeed distorted world.

In this struggle against the distorted world, however, religion plays a peculiar double role. On the one hand, and as Ludwig Feuerbach quite correctly recognized, it draws attention to the distorted world and to how human beings have in fact not yet attained their true reality. On the other hand, religion itself conceals from human beings their real situation by replacing true reality with fantastic reality. "Religious suffering is the expression of real suffering and at the same time the protest against real suffering. Religion is the sigh of the oppressed creature, the heart of

---

25. Karl Marx, *Selected Writings*, ed. Lawrence H. Simon (Indianapolis: Hackett, 1994), 28.

a heartless world. . . . It is the opium of the people."[26] Marx now insists that we not simply make do with a critique of religion. We must instead "unmask human self-alienation in its unholy forms now that it has been unmasked in its holy form. Thus the criticism of heaven turns into the criticism of the earth, the criticism of religion into the criticism of law, and the criticism of theology into the criticism of politics."[27]

Nietzsche's critique of religion similarly comes to its most imposing expression in its attack not merely on "priestly deception," which distracts human beings and fixates them on a world beyond by befogging them with empty and fantastic figures and beings. For he, too, expands his critique of religion into a comprehensive critique of culture and morals, attacking not only the notion of the protection of the weak as propagated by many religions and the political, legal, and moral commitment to an ethos of equality and freedom for all; he also makes religion responsible for the success of the kind of appellative morality through which emotionalized mass culture seeks to drag down to its own base level the more refined, sensitive, and subtle members of society. Nietzsche, however, is not yet thinking about the kind of symbolic religious kitsch that alienates so many reflective persons from religion today. Just as little is he thinking about the kind of cheap, self-righteous morality that laments the situation of the world and accuses the evil "others" of culpability in order to divert attention from its own lethargy and impotence and from its own failures in the face of quite concrete current situations of distress. Nonetheless, any self-critical critique of religion can certainly profit from

26. Marx, *Selected Writings*, 28.
27. Marx, *Selected Writings*, 28–29.

Nietzsche in becoming aware lest it similarly fall prey to such moralistic trends.[28]

Contra Nietzsche, however, theological critiques of religion must hold fast to the theological and ethical realism—with their accompanying truth claims—that Nietzsche himself perceived only in a distorted fashion and portrayed as blatant caricatures. Yet he does speak in a certain patronizing fashion about precisely such ethical realism when diagnosing it within the framework of the ethos of love inhering within the small Jewish family of the Diaspora:

> The reality upon which Christianity could build itself was the small *Jewish family* of the Diaspora, with its warmth and tenderness, with its readiness to help and to stand up for each other, unprecedented and perhaps uncomprehended in the whole of the Roman Empire ... with its unenvious saying No, deep within, to everything which has the upper hand and possesses power and magnificence. *To have recognized this as power*, to have recognized this *psychological* state as communicative, seductive, infectious for heathens too—that is the *genius* of Paul.[29]

Nietzsche explicates how Paul recognized as *power* the survival strategy of the "lower classes" he found before him—that is, the strategy of self-preservation of this "kind

28. See in this regard the contributions of Günter Thomas, *Gottes Lebendigkeit: Beiträge zur systematischen Theologie* (Leipzig: EVA, 2019), esp. chaps. 1, 9, 11, though see also Thomas, "Vertrauen und Risiko in moralischen Hoffnungsgrossprojekten," in *Risiko und Vertrauen*, 55–85.

29. Friedrich Nietzsche, *The Will to Power*, trans. Walter Kaufmann and R. J. Hollingdale, ed. Walter Kaufmann (New York: Vintage Books, 1968), 107, translation altered.

of person." Paul lucidly articulated this survival strategy as a strategy of "community self-preservation." And he initiated, "ignited" this strategy of self-preservation with the "principle of love."[30] I earlier drew attention in the third lecture to the radiant power that family ethos and religious ethos exert within the spirit of justice.

Like many other eminent theologians, so also did Dietrich Bonhoeffer draw self-critically from critiques of religion expressed outside theology proper. On July 8, 1944, he wrote in his letters from prison: "What I am driving at is that God should not be smuggled in somewhere in the very last, secret place that is left. . . . One must give up the 'holier-than-thou' ploys and not regard psychotherapy or existential philosophy as scouts preparing the way for God"—not to mention, of course, metaphysical speculation.[31]

Beginning in May 1944, Bonhoeffer developed an idea that would never quite leave him—namely, that of a life kept "multidimensional" and "polyphonic." He lamented the single-dimensionality and linearity characterizing the thinking of most people and remarked:

> Christianity, on the other hand, puts us into many different dimensions of life at the same time; in a way we accommodate God and the whole world within us. We weep with those who weep at the same time as we rejoice with those who rejoice. We fear . . . for our lives, but at the same time we must think thoughts that are much more important to us than our lives. . . . Life isn't

30. Nietzsche, *Will to Power*, 3, 571.
31. Dietrich Bonhoeffer, *Letters and Papers from Prison*, vol. 8 of *Dietrich Bonhoeffer Works*, trans. Isabel Best et al. (Minneapolis: Fortress, 2009), 457.

pushed back into a single dimension, but is kept multidimensional, polyphonic. What a liberation it is to be
able to *think* and to hold on to these many dimensions
of life in our thoughts. . . . One has to dislodge people
from their one-track thinking.[32]

Natural theology can similarly profit today by picking
up on this initiative to expand one's thinking by engaging
precisely this multimodal activity of the spirit. It should
similarly take seriously the philosophical and theological
critiques of religion that attack not only an exaggerated focus on the beyond but also religion itself in its role as the
initiator of distorted moral, social, intellectual, and cultural
developments and in alliance with such developments. One
key question for natural theology concerns the essence and
nature of God. The proposal in these lectures for addressing
this question can be articulated by translating a statement
from the theology of revelation into one commensurate
with the conceptual world of natural theology.

"God is spirit, and those who worship him must worship in spirit and truth." The Gospel of John attributes this
statement to Jesus himself (4:24) and associates it with the
discourse on prayer and worship. Let us leave in abeyance
for the moment the revelatory dimensions of this statement and consider seriously its initial words—namely, that
"God is spirit." That is, let us inquire in the sense of Lord
Gifford's intentions and within the framework of natural
theology concerning the anthropological and ethical resonance of this divine power. And above all let us consider, as

32. Bonhoeffer, *Letters and Papers from Prison*, 405; cf. Michael
Welker, *Theologische Profile: Schleiermacher, Barth, Bonhoeffer,
Moltmann*, Edition Chrismon (Frankfurt: Hansisches Druck- und
Verlagshaus, 2009), 116.

a mode of our search for truth, how one might in the light of the same spirit expand one's understanding of human beings as made in God's image.

Our previous findings are the following:

- Human beings are indeed made in God's image as destined seekers and practitioners of justice with an ethos of equality in a world replete with injustice and inequality.
- Human beings are indeed made in God's image in their destined commitment to freedom in both personal and social life circumstances in a world that presents countless hindrances to such freedom.
- Human beings are indeed made in God's image as destined seekers of truth and in their multifaceted if fragile efforts to attain and communicate in both thought and action an element of correctness, certitude, consensus, coherence, commensurability, and fertile and liberating knowledge.

In all these considerations, human beings are, on the one hand, beings gifted with earthly and transient life powers who, on the other hand, are destined to live from within the powers of the divine Spirit and in the process not only to gain a portion of these powers but also to communicate them to their fellow human beings and fellow creatures.

It is precisely this understanding that will be summarized and invoked in the sixth and final lecture—namely, human beings as being made in the image of God through their destined commitment to peace.

Lecture 6

CALLED TO PEACE

Many people understand "peace" to mean primarily the absence of war. Yet although almost all people fear war, opinions on how best to attain and secure peace can vary widely.

In the spring of 2019, the Stockholm International Peace Research Institute (SIPRI) published depressing statistics demonstrating that a disturbingly intense arms race is currently underway throughout the world. Indeed, it has been thirty years since arms expenditures were at this level. In the past ten years, China has increased its arms expenditures tenfold, while during the year 2019 alone the USA increased its arms expenditures by $50 billion, simultaneously cutting funds for development cooperation by almost the same amount. The (conservative) minister for economic aid in the Federal Republic of Germany, Gerd Müller, lamented that "if we could redirect even a quarter of military expenditures toward developmental cooperation, we could put a stop to hunger, death [i.e., death caused by severe conditions of distress and disaster], and poverty, as well as to the miseries of refugees worldwide. We must stop this disastrous cycle. Worldwide, about $1,600 billion go to the military, only $160 billion to development. Some day we will pay a high price for this disproportion."[1]

1. *Rhein-Neckar-Zeitung*, May 2, 2019, 19.

On *Eternal Peace*—Kant versus Vegetius

The Roman military theoretician Vegetius (late fourth century CE) coined the motto that was embraced by many states at the time and that many still embrace—namely, "*Si vis pacem, para bellum*" (If you want peace, prepare for war).

The great philosopher Immanuel Kant vehemently objected to this position in his famous publication *Eternal Peace*,[2] in which he argued that this view merely equates peace with a ceasefire. At the same time, however, Kant was certainly no rigid pacifist. He saw quite clearly that states need a border defense and must be in a position to oppose attacks from without. He does, however, challenge the notion that this goal can be attained solely by means of maximum armament, a perpetually expanding production of heavy weaponry, and the concomitant development and expansion of organized military power. Kant's key idea is that only conceptual and political efforts subordinated to the idea and praxis of the rule of law and justice can promote peace. The German philosopher Otfried Höffe has formulated this notion with elegant succinctness: "Kant opposes the essential thrust of Vegetius's motto 'Si vis pacem, para bellum' [If you want peace, prepare for war]

2. Kant's publication *Eternal Peace* (1795), sometimes translated as *Toward Perpetual Peace*, has been considered the high point not only of his own philosophy of history and politics but also of classical (sc. Western) bourgeois humanism. The initial print run of two thousand copies of this book, which Kant had delivered to his publisher in August 1795 and which had appeared a month later, was already sold out by December of that same year. It eventually became Kant's most successful publication during his lifetime, with a second printing during the first year of its publication and a second, revised edition during the following year (1796), along with ten more editions up till Kant's death in 1804.

114   IN GOD'S IMAGE

with the assertion 'Si vis pacem, para iustitiam' [If you want peace, ensure justice]."[3]

Not the power of violence and weapons but rather only the power of justice and politics that supports justice through subordination to it can secure the kind of peace that fundamentally excludes war and, by genuinely constituting "the end of all hostilities," merits being called "eternal" according to Kant.[4] Kant's essay, which takes the form of a contract, deals quite soberly with the doubts and questions concerning whether this concept is realistic in the first place and whether real politics genuinely can be subordinated in practice to the idea of justice.

Kant presents an ethical-moral, political, and legal process of inculcation in which the multimodal spirit of peace can unfold. To wit, people themselves—both the governed and the governing, friend and foe—are to be persuaded that this world can live without belligerent actions and the infinite misery and suffering that follow in their wake if all

3. Otfried Höffe, "Einleitung: Der Friede—ein vernachlässigtes Ideal," in *Immanuel Kant, Zum ewigen Frieden, Klassiker auslegen*, vol. 1, 3rd ed., ed. Otfried Höffe (Berlin: Akademie Verlag, 2011), 12. The basic notion of Flavius Vegetius Renatus (*De re militari*, foreword to book 3) can already be found in Plato (*Nomoi* VIII, after 352 BCE) and Cicero in a discourse contra Marcus Antonius before the Roman senate in January of 43 BCE.

4. Immanuel Kant, "Toward Perpetual Peace: A Philosophical Sketch," in *Toward Perpetual Peace and Other Writings on Politics, Peace, and History*, ed. Pauline Kleingeld, trans. David L. Colclasure (New Haven: Yale University Press, 2006), 67–68 (= Immanuel Kant, "Zum ewigen Frieden," in *Kants Werke: Akademie Textausgabe*, vol. 8: *Abhandlungen nach 1781* [Berlin: de Gruyter, 1968], 343): "No peace settlement which secretly reserves issues for a future war shall be considered valid. For such a treaty would represent a mere cease-fire, a postponement of hostilities, and not peace. For peace signifies the end to all hostilities, and even merely adding the adjective perpetual to the term renders it a suspicious-looking pleonasm."

people commit to live with one another under the rule of an ethically-morally shaped notion of justice.

Broad stretches of this document seem to be spoken directly to our own time rather than composed over two hundred years ago. Precisely by illuminating the intellectual-moral, material-natural, political, legal, and, not least, also the economic and medial framework necessary for a politics and ethos of peace, Kant's essay acquires an enduring, undiminished power of persuasion. On the basis of the following insights, Kant himself can be reckoned as a conceptual precursor of the charter of the United Nations of October 24, 1945 (especially in the preamble and articles 1 and 2):

1. The old idea of statesmanship was oriented toward perpetually expanding the power and territory of the state and was commensurately designed for expansion and aggression. Politics was satisfied with merely a truce that was called "peace" but that in principle made it possible to further state interest in expansion and aggression. Kant appealed to the "dignity of a ruler" and to "the true honor of the state" to desist fundamentally and enduringly from this attitude.[5]

2. If you want peace, then appreciate and foster your own freedom and that of others. Any politics of peace must respect the sovereignty of states and the freedom of their citizens. Military cooperation between states and the mustering of citizens for defense come about only when states agree in a specific case to the self-defense of a given state against external aggression. Any politics of peace must also take

5. Kant, *Perpetual Peace*, 68 (Akademie Ausgabe 8:344).

       measures to put a stop to economically exploitative relationships between states and to all forms of violent intrusion and terrorist activity.

3.   With respect to organized military entities, the commitment to a rigorous politics of peace requires at least the gradual elimination of "standing armies" (*miles perpetuus*)[6] and at least the gradual dismantling of competitive expansions of armaments between states.

For our age, too, these demands remain an enormous, challenging task for all humankind, comparable to the struggle for egalitarian justice and freedom and against ecological brutality and global climate destruction. Although the conversion of armament industries from their primary production of destructive weaponry into politically and ecologically creative technological instruments of peace requires that we all take a deep breath of patience and hope, nonetheless precisely this transition should be initiated on an international basis and with appropriate efficiency controls. Nor should the acknowledgment be delayed that the best long-term way to secure borders and ensure the peaceful organization of states and the increasingly multinational and multiethnic composition of their populations is not through walls and destructive weaponry but solely through creative external developmental assistance alongside responsible domestic policies of education and integration.

As Kant himself emphasizes, the prerequisite for actualizing this vision is the implementation of legal and constitutional measures that guarantee the freedom and equality of all citizens, secure respect for justice and the law, and

6. Kant, *Perpetual Peace*, 67 (Akademie Ausgabe 8:343).

stabilize the division of political power between the executive and legislative branches of government.[7] International goals include the establishment of a federal alliance of states and the development of international law, to be complemented by the propagation of human rights. The indispensable foundation of this national and international order of peace is the development of the appropriate legal and moral thinking and the concomitant understanding of politics along with, as Kant puts it, "publicity," which we today associate with the power of education, science and scholarship, and the media, and of which the transparency of action constitutes an essential part. "All actions that affect the rights of other human beings, the maxims of which are incompatible with publicity, are unjust."[8]

- If you want peace, then promote respect for the truth and a commitment to communication that seeks the truth. This requirement is inherent in Kant's demand that actions relating to the rights of others be compatible with publicity.
- If you want peace, then appreciate and promote your own freedom and that of others.
- If you want peace, then ensure justice.

The extent to which the multimodal spirit of peace is interwoven in a variety of ways with the multimodal spirit of justice, freedom, and truth becomes quite clear in these considerations.

Yet the political, legal, and moral framework for any

7. Kant, *Perpetual Peace*, "First Definitive Article of a Perpetual Peace: The Civil Constitution of Every State Shall Be Republican," 76 (Akademie Ausgabe 8:352).

8. Kant, *Perpetual Peace*, 104 (Akademie Ausgabe 8:381).

enduring thwarting of belligerent activities and for supporting the urgently needed efforts to prompt the concrete transition of the armaments industry—currently focused on maximum destructive capacity—to a political framework focused on peace, constitute but one aspect of the multimodal spirit of peace. For *how* are people to be persuaded to withdraw their loyalty from the politics of a spiraling arms race? *How* exactly can one ignite a passionate interest in them for "eternal peace"? Which *sources* might nourish such commitment and courage for eternal peace?

Peace as an Internally Human and Civilizational Disposition

In his book *Adventures of Ideas*,[9] Alfred North Whitehead asked about the "essential qualities, whose joint realization in social life constitutes civilization." In his opinion, these qualities are "Truth, Beauty, Adventure, Art."[10] He asks further how the pursuit of these qualities might be kept from becoming "ruthless, hard, [and] cruel." The solution is to be found in a "Harmony of Harmonies, [which] shall bind together the other four qualities [i.e., Truth, Beauty, Adventure, and Art], so as to exclude from our notion of civilization the restless egotism with which they have often in fact been pursued. . . . I choose the term 'Peace' for that Harmony of Harmonies which calms destructive turbulence and completes civilization."[11]

9. Alfred North Whitehead, *Adventures of Ideas* (New York: Free Press, 1967).

10. Whitehead, *Adventures of Ideas*, 284.

11. Whitehead, *Adventures of Ideas*, 285.

Whitehead defines the spirit of peace as "a broadening of feeling" that generates a remarkable loss of self and an equally remarkable expansion of self, of the person, or of the social entity that focuses on peace. Peace "results in a wider sweep of conscious interest. It enlarges the field of attention." It focuses on "coördinations," concurrences between human beings that "are wider than personality" or than any single initiative for peace from whatever source.[12] Whitehead discerns quite clearly the self-endangerment that individual persons and social entities risk who want nothing more than to continue with proven structures of self-preservation and self-development and who as a result end up losing—gradually, in a creeping fashion—the capacity to be surprised and the intensity of feeling and emotion. The depth and breadth of their capacity for experience diminish; they themselves atrophy—be it at ever so lofty a level. Their world steadily shrinks and becomes steadily more impoverished and insignificant.

Whitehead counters this notion by proposing peace as "the intuition of permanence," a condition fulfilled only by conditions of the soul and the world that as "an abiding perfection" enter into "the nature of things, a treasure for all ages."[13]

Although this vision of peace as a creative process that transcends primary interests in simple self-relationships and self-preservation may seem rather vague and effusive, it does nonetheless offer a perspective from which to discern insufficient or inadequate notions of peace. Such notions variously mistake peace, for example, for tranquility, order, and security. For after all, even those who perpetrate extraordinarily repressive or even terroristic

12. Whitehead, *Adventures of Ideas*, 285.
13. Whitehead, *Adventures of Ideas*, 285, 291.

circumstances can boast about the regnance of tranquility, order, and security within their own spheres of influence—for example, the assertion that "under apartheid the streets in Cape Town were quiet during the evening." One could, of course, hear similar asseverations in Germany under Hitler.

In book 19 of *De civitate Dei*, Augustine presents a lofty doctrine of peace focused on the idea of a social order that ensures calm and justice.[14] Although Augustine can also understand peace as the absence of strife (19.10.27) and as undisturbed calm (19.12.14), such "undisturbed order" can just as easily derive from the cemetery calm of repression.[15] Augustine is intent on articulating the idea of peace at a deeper level. Probably picking up initiatives from Cicero and the Stoics, he associates peace with "undisturbed order" in which justice reigns.[16] Rüdiger Bittner maintains that Augustine here adopts the Stoic view that "order as objective justice" constitutes a "fundamental characteristic of the world." Augustine then externally refers this empirically sooner unpersuasive view to God as the "governor" of this order (19.12.13). But this view in its own turn merely obscures the difficulties accompanying any linking of a sus-

---

14. Augustine, *S. Augustin's City of God (De civitate Dei) and Christian Doctrine, A Select Library of the Nicene and Post-Nicene Fathers of the Christian Church*, vol. 2, ed. Philip Schaff (Edinburgh: T&T Clark, 1887). See Rüdiger Bittner, "Augustinus über Frieden," in *Gegenwart des lebendigen Christus*, 479–95.

15. Eberhard Jüngel, "Zum Wesen des Friedens. Frieden als Kategorie theologischer Anthropologie," in Eberhard Jüngel, *Ganz werden: Theologische Erörterungen V* (Tübingen: Mohr Siebeck, 2003), 12: "By 'peace' Augustine understands . . . ordered circumstances free of all disturbances."

16. See Bittner, "Augustinus über Frieden," 489.

tainable understanding of peace with a persuasive program for the realization of justice.

The difficulties we encountered in the third lecture with the now "dull" instrument of natural law catch up with Augustine here. An inherent but unrealistic "just order" is attributed to the world and nature with God as its guarantor and with "sweet peace" ultimately being displaced into a heavenly "beyond" (19.17). But without the powers of the spirit, neither nature nor the world provides any reliable foundations for peace and justice. And without the powers of the spirit, so also do the powers of God remain mysterious and obscure.

How, then, are such powers of the spirit of peace to be comprehended in a sufficiently *realistic* fashion for an individual person? Whitehead refers not only to the harmonies residing in "Truth, Beauty, Adventure, and Art" but also explicitly to an element considerably more accessible to human experience and to the individual's capacity for exerting formative influence than are the largely aesthetic forms associated with the harmonies. To wit, he associates the movement of self-transcending in the direction of experiential peace with the experience of the giving and receiving of love, especially as the latter are associated with intimate and caring parental love. This love is above all a love that serves the carefree development of the beloved counterpart. Whitehead himself refers to the "love of self-devotion where the potentialities of the loved [counterpart] are felt passionately as a claim that it find itself in a friendly Universe."[17] This insight does indeed open up the possibility of a more profound experience of peace.

---

17. Whitehead, *Adventures of Ideas*, 289. Whitehead in fact uses the term "object" rather than "counterpart" so as to include not only human beings but also other creatures and even aesthetic objects.

Benevolence toward Humankind and Shared Joy:
On True Inner Peace

This sort of solicitous, caring love that wants only the best for the beloved and that seeks but to contribute in a considered and farsighted fashion to that person's free development such "that it find itself in a friendly Universe" is a magical power transcending far more than merely one's own natural interest in self-preservation. For by seeking to serve the free self-development of the beloved, it also overcomes to whatever extent possible its own natural tendencies for control and imposition. This inclination runs quite counter to our tendencies toward natural self-preservation as well as to tendencies for loving care in continuity solely with our own self-preservation. I have come to refer to this inclination as "free creative self-limitation and self-withdrawal on behalf of others."[18]

This expression refers to a radical movement of self-transcendence that cannot really be grasped through the simple notion of selflessness.[19] The reference is instead to a vital energy and a life beyond the usual understanding of natural vital energy, which is inherently and indispensably linked to self-continuation and self-preservation. Through giving and receiving this love, a person acquires even in this life a portion of the "eternal life" that points beyond natural-earthly life circumstances.

This love responds to the question Martha Nussbaum formulated in *Upheavals of Thought* as follows: "How, then, can love reform itself, so as not to be excessively

18. Welker, *God the Spirit*, 248–58; Michael Welker, *God the Revealed: Christology*, trans. Douglas Stott (Grand Rapids: Eerdmans, 2013), 223–34.

19. Thus Ted Peters, "Entheokaric Freedom: Clarifying Confusions," in *Risiko und Vertrauen = Risk and Trust*, 339–48.

needy, vengeful, or partial, and so as to be supportive of general social compassion, reciprocity, and respect for individuality?"[20] In an assessment of the works of numerous thinkers, poets, and even of a composer, Nussbaum seeks answers to this question concerning appropriate "ascents of love," albeit without finding clear, comprehensive answers.[21]

Studies by Martin Nowak and other evolutionary theoreticians have shown that not only mutation and selection but also cooperation plays a key role in success within evolutionary history. Indeed, cooperation takes place even at the cellular level. Where such cooperation collapses and cells "revert to their primitive program of selfish replication," destructive and deadly processes begin.[22] "Cancer is a breakdown of cooperation." Evolutionary success through cooperation is characterized by reciprocal processes accompanied by calculated assessments of cost and usefulness, though also by sooner unquantifiable enhancements to the reputation of individuals and groups. Nowak observes that "the recent appreciation of the importance of evolution of cooperation shifts the perspective of evolution from a purely competitive scenario to one that includes the possibility of cooperation and altruism. More than this,

20. Martha C. Nussbaum, *Upheavals of Thought: The Intelligence of Emotions* (Cambridge: Cambridge University Press, 2001), 481.

21. Nussbaum engages a variety of perspectives in surveying works by Plato, Aristophanes, Spinoza, Proust, Augustine, Dante, Brontë, Whitman, Joyce, and Mahler (*Upheavals of Thought*, 457–714).

22. Martin A. Nowak, "God and Evolution," in *The Science and Religion Dialogue*, 49; see also Martin A. Nowak, *Evolutionary Dynamics: Exploring the Equations of Life* (Cambridge: Harvard University Press, 2006); Martin A. Nowak, *Super Cooperators: Why We Need Each Other to Succeed* (New York: Free Press, 2011).

one can argue that cooperation is needed for constructing higher levels of organization in the biological world."[23]

Sarah Coakley picked up these initiatives in her 2012 Gifford Lectures in Aberdeen with the title "Sacrifice Regained: Evolution, Cooperation and God." In her sixth lecture, "Reconceiving 'Natural Theology': Meaning, Sacrifice and God," she advocated the notion of "altruism beyond calculation," which she considers motivated ultimately by Christology and a theology of the cross. She engages images of the resurrection to evoke what she calls a "positive and affective commitment"[24] based on religious and aesthetic powers. The question now is how one can accommodate these scientific and religious concerns to universal and, in this sense, natural human experiences and to an ascertainable sense of inner peace.

Coakley has maintained that every pregnancy and every birth is associated with creative self-withdrawal on behalf of new life and to that extent also with the notion of "sacrifice." An illuminating study by Sigrid Brandt has opened our eyes to the fact that because some languages do *not* distinguish between "sacrifice" and "victim," they ineluctably suggest the notion of inevitable victimization within sacrifice.[25] This circumstance has prompted a great many highly problematical and erroneous theological and ideological developments. Yet even though some births do indeed result in life-threatening situations or even in death, the sacrifice of pregnancy and birth should *not* for that reason necessarily be associated with victimization. In intact

23. Nowak, "God and Evolution," 49.

24. Sarah Coakley, "Sacrifice Regained: Evolution, Cooperation and God," 2012 Gifford Lectures, https://www.giffordlectures.org/lecturers/sarah-coakley.

25. Sigrid Brandt, *Opfer als Gedächtnis: Auf dem Weg zu einer befreienden theologischen Rede von Opfer* (Münster: LIT, 2001).

natural and political life circumstances, the resulting new life enriches the mother, the family, and the world, and in this sense the attempts of Brandt and Coakley to encourage "liberating discourse about sacrifice," especially Brandt's arguments for a deeper understanding of sacrifice without victimization, are of inestimable value.

Because references to "sacrifice" and even "love" often exhibit dramatic and out-of-the-ordinary connotations, they can be associated with "peace" only to a limited extent. Distinguishing between hot, warm, cool, and cold emotions can help impose order on the world of feelings. Cold emotions are generally dying or dead emotions that in a sense simply play themselves out. In contrast, many stronger aesthetic emotions can be called hot emotions. In popular culture, electronic transmissions through the media of elite athletic competitions and of musical entertainment represent unmistakable examples of efforts to generate hot emotions. Romantic love in the guise of one-sided yearning or as mutually reciprocal love is and will always remain hot and exciting. Although the depth of devotion associated with kenotic love that is ever willing to make sacrifices is often quite moving, it can also take on forbidding and threatening forms. By contrast, we tend to perceive the love between partners and friends as "warm," as it were as iterations of covenantal love in which people remain loyal through thick and thin. But it is only in limited spheres of life that people can experience these various forms of love.[26] And it is not "hot" but rather only "warm" love of the sort we both give and experience within the intimate sphere of parental love that can be associated with "inner peace."

26. Michael Welker, "Romantic Love, Covenantal Love, Kenotic Love," in *The Work of Love: Creation as Kenosis*, ed. J. Polkinghorne (Grand Rapids: Eerdmans; London: SPCK, 2001), 127–36.

The grand magical power that turns love into a universal power of both internal and external peace resides beyond the powers of warm love within what one might call the cool and calm love of benevolence toward humankind that wishes only good and never ill to one's fellow human beings. This love is ever willing to engage both in cooperation and, within limits, in creative self-withdrawal on behalf of fellow creatures. It does not constantly calculate the balance of cost-usefulness. The potential for its own self-development does not represent a constant stimulus for it. Instead, it provides space for others and then is glad when it, too, is granted space for development and forward movement.

This cool and calm love of benevolence toward humankind can, of course, intensify to more emphatic forms of love. It can become more excited, warmer, and hotter, indeed even to the point of restricting or bringing to an end one's sense of peace. But the sense of calm, shared joy that accompanies the warm and cool and calm forms of love invariably secures and enhances one's sense of peace. In this context, it is important that joy be acknowledged and appreciated not only in its more overt, effusive, jubilant forms but also in its quiet or even cool, self-forgetful manifestations. Indeed, given this broad spectrum of manifestations, one might even speak of a polyphony of joy.

A project initiated by the Heidelberg Academy of Science and Humanities on the biology and opportunities associated with aging conducted interdisciplinary studies on the life experiences and feelings of people at advanced ages, including those at extremely advanced ages accompanied by dramatically increasing fragility and approaching death.[27] Are such situations of increasingly compromised

27. The present discussion references the conference "Altern:

health and physical capacity necessarily characterized solely by the cold feeling of purported peace only in the sense of the peace and quiet of the cemetery? Or can one articulate a substantive understanding of peace whose resilience endures when subjected to real-life experience?

The observation has often been made that people in the pianissimo of advanced and extremely advanced age can become like small children. Children and young people, however, can grow and develop as they should only through the care others devote to them. In precisely this situation they learn that other people are there for them, people who lovingly withdraw from their own concerns on their behalf. That is, children and young people live within a life context that for those who care for them is oriented toward "free, creative self-withdrawal and self-limitation on their behalf."[28]

This experience of the self-withdrawal and self-limitation of others on their behalf generates, consciously or unconsciously, not only feelings of gratitude and affection among such children and young people but also the expectation and hope that those others will continue and renew this behavior and attitude. This combination of gratitude and hope nourishes a profound sense of joy and peace that comes to expression in numerous manifestations, both emphatic and quiet. This experience of joy and peace is, of course, to be anticipated more in concentrated social circumstances that include friends and family, even if occasionally here, too, disappointment and alienation remain possible. But it is not only the vitality of such a social

Biologie und Chancen" (2019/2020) containing my own contribution, "Dein Alter sei wie deine Jugend: Impulse eines Segensworts."

28. Welker, *God the Spirit*, 248–58; Welker, *God the Revealed*, 223–34.

environment but also the world of individual recollection and kinship with nature or the rhythms of the day and year that can serve as fertile sources of joy and a sense of peace, especially at an advanced age with its more pronounced experiences of fragility and finitude.

For even amid diminishing physical and spiritual-intellectual powers, gratitude and hope generate feelings of strength accompanied by joy. The phenomenon of shared joy with its accompanying sense of peace was strikingly evident in evaluations of the feelings of aging citizens in Germany. Andreas Kruse confirmed these observations in many publications and many important empirical studies.[29] Interviews in this context disclosed the preferred frameworks for dealing with what are known as "themes of existence." The highest-ranking framework was "joy and fulfillment in an emotionally fulfilling encounter with others." Another notably preferred context was a concentration on the next generation, which though understandably especially intensive in one's own family nonetheless also came to strong expression in contexts far transcending that sphere.

Such concentration can but must not necessarily intensify in connection with a person's capacity to contribute something to that next generation on an emotional-communicative or material-practical level. That is, the capacity to transcend one's own life burdens in creative self-withdrawal on behalf of others provides a powerful source of experiential joy and profound inner peace.[30] This

29. Andreas Kruse, *Lebensphase hohes Alter: Verletzlichkeit und Reife* (Berlin: Springer Verlag, 2017); Generali Deutschland AG, ed., *Generali Altersstudie 2017: Wie ältere Menschen in Deutschland denken und leben* (Frankfurt a.M.: Fischer Verlag, 2012; Berlin: Springer Verlag, 2017), chap. 4.

30. Miroslav Volf has over the years emphasized the enormous

experience of peace resides securely and reliably within the warm love toward others in one's immediate sphere as well as in the cool and calm love toward others quite beyond any ethos associated with intimate spheres, and through precisely this engagement that same experience acquires a beneficent radiance and resonance even at the very boundaries of life's natural energies.

Conclusion

I have tried in these six lectures to develop a natural theology of the human and divine spirit. At the very outset, we ascertained that human finitude and frailty, and especially human seductibility and massive forms of collective self-endangerment, aggressivity, and destructive inclinations, profoundly call into question any references to human beings as having been created "in the image of God." The five subsequent lectures then inquired concerning what powers of the human and divine spirit might counter this discouraging state of affairs.

The examination of the natural, cultural, and religious potential of the multimodal human and divine spirit presented in the second lecture opened perspectives capable of bringing into focus a realistic natural theology.

People filled by the multimodal spirit of justice become capable of engaging on behalf of justice in both word and deed in a world characterized by radically inequitable and

---

powers of forgiveness and joy: *Free of Charge: Giving and Forgiving in a Culture Stripped of Grace* (Grand Rapids: Zondervan, 2005); *Flourishing: Why We Need Religion in a Globalized World* (New Haven: Yale University Press, 2016); Miroslav Volf and Justin Crisp, eds., *Joy and Human Flourishing: Essays on Theology, Culture and the Good Life* (Minneapolis: Fortress, 2015).

unjust life circumstances. Precisely thus, such people are indeed called and shaped in the image of God.

They are similarly shaped in the image of God when the multimodal spirit of freedom fills them and gives them the power to fight for liberation and freedom morally, legally, politically, and in countless educational contexts in a world replete with personal and social manifestations of repression and the lack of freedom.

People are similarly shaped in the image of God when, filled by the multimodal spirit of truth, they struggle to bring truth to bear critically and self-critically on the many levels of the search for truth. In the spirit of truth, they practice resolute advocacy and defense of convincingly argued and empirically tested truth claims. And not least, these people recognize the inner connections between the activities of the spirit as the spirit of truth, freedom, and justice.

These interrelated contexts in which the multimodal spirit is engaged come to concentrated expression once more in its manifestation as the spirit of peace and in the shaping of human beings into the image of God within the peaceful struggle against those powers that try to promote a spirit of hostility, hatred, and warmongering. In the form of the warm love of family, friends, and those in our immediate surroundings, and in the form of a cool and calm universal benevolence toward all humankind, the spirit of peace acquires its overwhelming radiant and resonating power.

The natural-theological perspectives on the shaping of human beings in the image of God can also be articulated with respect to secular contexts. In the third lecture I reflected on the spirit of justice that activates the powers of political, legal, religious, and familial ethos as well as numerous resources of empathy with which one might engage on behalf of justice and equality in a world characterized by radically inequitable and unjust life circumstances. In the fourth lecture I suggested that this spirit of justice must, however, be accompanied by the multimodal spirit of freedom to facilitate the emergence of appropriate forms of personal, moral, and political existence in freedom and dignity. The fifth lecture demonstrated that the multimodal spirit of truth must ensure an informative critical and self-critical assessment of cultural and moral circumstances in society and provides impetus for a more expansive and penetrating understanding of human existence.

The sixth lecture has demonstrated that the spirit of peace relates all these impulses within an ethos focused nationally and internationally on justice, freedom, and on science, scholarship, education, and communicative media that are resolutely committed to truth, thereby awakening and sustaining within both personal and interpersonal life a spirit of warm and cool and calm love and of the profound joy that accompanies such love.

It is in this spirit of peace and in love that every individual person and all humankind are elevated to the dignity that comprehends all humanity and are genuinely equipped with the powers necessary for living commensurate with this grand destiny: in the image of God.

Bibliography

Abramowitz, Michael J. "Freedom in the World 2018: Democracy in Crisis." In Freedom House, *Freedom in the World 2018: The Annual Survey of Political Rights and Civil Liberties*, 1–9. New York: Rowman, 2019.

Arendt, Hannah. *Essays in Understanding, 1930–1954*. Edited by Jerome Kohn. Translated by Robert Kimber and Rita Kimber. New York: Harcourt Brace Jovanovich, 1994.

———. "The Freedom to Be Free." In Hannah Arendt, *Thinking without a Banister: Essays in Understanding*, vol. 11, edited by Jerome Kohn, 368–94. New York: Schocken Books, 2018.

———. *The Human Condition*. 2nd ed. Chicago: University of Chicago Press, 1998.

———. *The Life of the Mind*. Vol. 1, *Thinking*. Vol. 2, *Willing*. 2 vols. in 1. New York: Harcourt Brace Jovanovich, 1978.

———. *On Violence*. New York: Houghton Mifflin Harcourt, 1970.

———. *The Origins of Totalitarianism*. 2nd ed. New York: Harcourt Brace Jovanovich, 1958. German edition: *Elemente und Ursprünge totaler Herrschaft: Antisemitismus, Imperialismus, totale Herrschaft*. 20th ed. München, Berlin, Zürich: Piper, 2017.

———. *Thinking without a Banister: Essays in Understanding*. Vol. 11. Edited by Jerome Kohn. New York: Schocken Books, 2018.

Aristotle. *Metaphysica*. Vol. 8 of *The Works of Aristotle*. Translated by W. D. Ross. Oxford: Clarendon, 1928.

Assmann, Jan. *Ma'at: Gerechtigkeit und Unsterblichkeit im Alten Ägypten*. Munich: Beck, 1990.

Augustine. *The City of God*. Vol. 1 of *The Works of Aurelius Augustine*. Edited by Marcus Dods. Edinburgh: T&T Clark, 1871.

———. *S. Augustin's City of God (De civitate Dei) and Christian Doctrine*. In *A Select Library of the Nicene and Post-Nicene Fathers of the Christian Church*, vol. 2, ed. Philip Schaff. Edinburgh: T&T Clark, 1887.

Aulfinger, Michael. *Urukagina, der gerechte König*. Neckenmarkt: Edition Nove, 2007.

Barbour, Ian. *Religion in an Age of Science: The Gifford Lectures 1989–1991*. Vol. 1. San Francisco: Harper, 1990.

Bedford-Strohm, Heinrich. *Gemeinschaft aus kommunikativer Freiheit: Sozialer Zusammenhalt in der modernen Gesellschaft. Ein theologischer Beitrag*. Gütersloh: Gütersloher Verlagshaus, 1999.

Bieri, Peter. *Das Handwerk der Freiheit: Über die Entdeckung des eigenen Willens*. Munich: Hanser 2001.

Bird, Phyllis. "'Male and Female He Created Them': Gen 1:27b in the Context of the Priestly Account of Creation." *Harvard Theological Review* 74 (1981): 129–59.

Bittner, Rüdiger. "Augustinus über Frieden." In *Gegenwart des lebendigen Christus*, edited by Günter Thomas and Andreas Schüle, 479–95. Leipzig: EVA, 2007.

———. *Bürger sein: Eine Prüfung politischer Begriffe*. Munich: de Gruyter, 2017.

———. "What It Is to Be Free." In *Quests for Freedom: Biblical, Historical, Contemporary*, 2nd ed., edited by Michael Welker, 98–114. Eugene, OR: Wipf & Stock, 2019.

———. "Without Laws." In *Concepts of Law in the Sciences, Legal Studies, and Theology*, edited by Michael Welker and Gregor Etzelmüller, 339–53. Tübingen: Mohr Siebeck, 2013.

Bonhoeffer, Dietrich. *Letters and Papers from Prison*. Vol. 8 of *Dietrich Bonhoeffer Works*. Translated by Isabel Best et al. Minneapolis: Fortress, 2009.

Brandt, Sigrid. *Opfer als Gedächtnis: Auf dem Weg zu einer befreienden theologischen Rede von Opfer*. Münster: LIT, 2001.

Brown, Warren, Nancey Murphy, and H. Newton Malony, eds. *Whatever Happened to the Soul? Scientific and Theological Portraits of Human Nature*. Philadelphia: Fortress, 1998.

Butler, Judith. *Bodies That Matter: On the Discursive Limits of "Sex."* London: Routledge Classics, 2011.

———. "My Life, Your Life: Equality and the Philosophy of Non-Violence." Gifford Lectures, Glasgow, 2018. https://www.giffordlectures.org/lecturers/judith-butler-0.

Coakley, Sarah. "Sacrifice Regained: Evolution, Cooperation and God." 2012 Gifford Lectures. https://www.giffordlectures.org/lecturers/sarah-coakley.

The Code of Hammurabi. Translated by Theophile J. Meek. In *Ancient Near Eastern Texts Relating to the Old Testament*, 3rd ed., edited by James B. Pritchard, 163–80. Princeton: Princeton University Press, 1969.

Dalferth, Ingolf. *Naturrecht in protestantischer Perspektive*. Würzburger Vorträge zur Rechtsphilosophie, Rechtstheorie und Rechtssoziologie 38. Baden-Baden: Nomos, 2008.

Diessel, Holger. "Deixis and Demonstratives." In *An International Handbook of Natural Language Meaning*, vol. 3, edited by Claudia Maienborn, Klaus von Heusinger, and Paul Portner, 2407–31. Berlin: de Gruyter, 2012.

Elshtain, Jean Bethke. *Sovereignty: God, State, and Self*. New York: Basic Books, 2008.

Fensham, F. Ch. "Widow, Orphan, and the Poor in Ancient Near Eastern Legal and Wisdom Literature." *Journal of Near Eastern Studies* 21 (1962): 129–39.

Fergusson, David. "Humans Created according to the IMAGO DEI: An Alternative Proposal." *Zygon* 48 (2013): 439–53.

———. *The Providence of God: A Polyphonic Approach*. Cambridge: Cambridge University Press, 2018.

Fuentes, Agustín. "Why We Believe: Evolution, Making Meaning, and the Development of Human Nature," https://www.giffordlectures.org/lecturers/agust%C3%ADn-fuentes.

Gallagher, Shaun. *How the Body Shapes the Mind*. Oxford: Clarendon, 2006.

Generali Deutschland AG, ed. *Generali Altersstudie 2017. Wie ältere Menschen in Deutschland denken und leben*. Berlin: Springer Verlag, 2017.

Gerhardt, Volker. "In Vergessenheit geraten: Über die Unverzichtbarkeit der Wahrheit." *Forschung und Lehre* 24 (2017): 754–56.

Goshen-Gottstein, Alon, ed. *Friendship across Religions: Theological Perspectives on Interreligious Friendship*. Eugene, OR: Wipf & Stock, 2018.

Gregersen, Niels Henrik, Willem B. Drees, and Ulf Görman, eds. *The Human Person in Science and Theology*. Edinburgh: T&T Clark, 2000.

Gregersen, Niels Henrik, and Wentzel Van Huyssteen. *Rethinking Theology and Science: Six Models for the Current Dialogue*. Grand Rapids: Eerdmans, 1998.

Habermas, Jürgen. *Between Facts and Norms: Contributions to a Discourse Theory of Law and Democracy*. Cambridge, MA: MIT Press, 1996.

————. *Philosophical-Political Profiles.* Cambridge, MA: MIT Press, 1983.

Halfwassen, Jens. "Gott im Denken: Warum die Philosophie auf die Frage nach Gott nicht verzichten kann." In *Gott—Götter—Götzen: XIV. Europäischer Kongress für Theologie,* Veröffentlichungen der Wissenschaftlichen Gesellschaft für Theologie, vol. 38, edited by Christoph Schwöbel, 187–96. Leipzig: EVA, 2013.

Harakas, Stanley. "Human Rights: An Eastern Orthodox Perspective." *Journal of Ecumenical Studies* 19 (1982): 13–26.

Härle, Wilfried. "Das christliche Verständnis der Wahrheit." In *Wahrheit, Marburger Jahrbuch Theologie,* vol. 21, edited by Wilfried Härle and Rainer Breuel, 61–89. Leipzig: EVA, 2009.

Harris, Mark. "The Biblical Text and a Functional Account of the *Imago Dei.*" In *Finding Ourselves after Darwin: Conversations on the Image of God, Original Sin, and the Problem of Evil,* edited by Stanley Rosenberg, 48–63. Grand Rapids: Baker Academic, 2018.

Hegel, G. W. F. "Differenz des Fichte'schen und Schelling'schen Systems der Philosophie." In G. W. F. Hegel, *Jenaer Kritische Schriften, Gesammelte Werke,* vol. 4, edited by Hartmut Buchner and Otto Pöggeler, 1–92. Hamburg: Felix Meiner, 1968.

————. *Elements of the Philosophy of Right.* Edited by Allen W. Wood. Translated by H. B. Nisbet. Cambridge: Cambridge University Press, 1991.

————. "Fragmente einer Kritik der Verfassung Deutschlands." In G. W. F. Hegel, *Gesammelte Werke,* vol. 5, *Schriften und Entwürfe (1799–1808),* edited by Manfred Baum and Kurt Rainer Meist, 1–24. Hamburg: Felix Meiner, 1998.

————. *Frühe Schriften, Werke 1.* Theorie Werkausgabe. Frankfurt: Suhrkamp Verlag, 1971.

————. "Glauben und Wissen." In G. W. F. Hegel, *Jenaer Kritische Schriften, Gesammelte Werke,* vol. 4, edited by Hartmut Buchner and Otto Pöggeler, 313–414. Hamburg: Felix Meiner, 1968.

————. *Hegels theologische Jugendschriften.* Edited by Herman Nohl. Tübingen: J. C. B. Mohr Siebeck, 1907. Reprint, Verlag der Wissenschaften, 2018. English translation: *Early Theological Writings.* Translated by T. M. Knox and Richard Kroner. Philadelphia: University of Pennsylvania Press, 1975, 8th ed., 1996.

————. *Hegel: The Letters.* Translated by Clark Butler and Christiane Seiler. Bloomington: Indiana University Press, 1984.

————. *On Christianity: Early Theological Writings.* Translated by T. M. Knox and Richard Kroner. New York: Harper Torchbooks, 1961.

————. *Phänomenologie des Geistes, Gesammelte Werke,* vol. 9, edited by Wolfgang Bonsiepen and Reinhard Heede. Hamburg: Felix Meiner, 1980. English translation: *The Phenomenology of Spirit.* Translated by Terry Pinkard. Cambridge: Cambridge University Press, 2019.

————. *Three Essays, 1793–1795: The Tubingen Essay, Berne Fragments, The Life of Jesus by G. W. F. Hegel.* Translated by Peter Fuss and John Dobbins. Notre Dame, IN: University of Notre Dame Press, 1984. https://www.scribd.com/document/227694655/Life-of-Jesus-Das-Leben-Jesu-G-W-F-Hegel.

Henrich, Dieter. *Hegel im Kontext.* Frankfurt: Suhrkamp, 1971; new ed. Berlin: Suhrkamp, 2010.

Höffe, Otfried. "Einleitung: Der Friede—ein vernachlässigtes Ideal." In *Immanuel Kant, Zum ewigen Frieden,*

Klassiker auslegen, vol. 1, 3rd ed., edited by Otfried Höffe, 1–19. Berlin: Akademie Verlag, 2011.

Höhl, Stefanie. "Frühkindliches Lernen in sozialen Interaktionen. Welche Rolle spielt Verkörperung?" In *Verkörperung: Eine neue interdisziplinäre Anthropologie*, edited by Gregor Etzelmüller, Thomas Fuchs, and Christian Tewes, 33–55. Berlin: de Gruyter, 2017.

Huber, Wolfgang. *Ethik: Grundfragen unseres Lebens*. Munich: Beck, 2013.

———. *Von der Freiheit: Perspektiven für eine solidarische Welt*. Munich: Beck, 2012.

Hurd, Elizabeth Shakman, and Winnifred Fallers Sullivan. "Symposium: Re-Thinking Religious Freedom, Editors' Introduction." *Journal of Law and Religion* 29 (2014): 358–62.

Ignatieff, Michael. *The Lesser Evil: Political Ethics in an Age of Terror*. Edinburgh: Edinburgh University Press, 2005.

The Institutes of Justinian. In *The Roman World*, vol. 3 of *The Library of Original Sources*, edited by Oliver J. Thatcher, 100–166. Milwaukee: University Research Extension, 1907.

Iverson, Jana M., and Susan Goldin-Meadow. "Gesture Paves the Way for Language Development." *Psychological Science* 16 (2005): 367–71.

Janowski, Bernd. *Anthropologie des Alten Testaments: Grundlagen—Kontexte—Themenfelder*. Tübingen: Mohr Siebeck, 2019.

Jarausch, Konrad H. *Broken Lives: How Ordinary Germans Experienced the Twentieth Century*. Princeton: Princeton University Press, 2018.

Jaster, Romy, and David Lanius. *Die Wahrheit schafft sich ab: Wie Fake News Politik machen*. 2nd ed. Stuttgart: Reclam, 2019.

Jeeves, Malcolm, ed. *From Cells to Souls—and Beyond: Chang-*

ing Portraits of Human Nature. Grand Rapids: Eerdmans, 2004.

Jüngel, Eberhard. "Zum Wesen des Friedens. Frieden als Kategorie theologischer Anthropologie." In *Ganz werden: Theologische Erörterungen V*, 1–39. Tübingen: Mohr Siebeck, 2003.

Kant, Immanuel. *Critique of Practical Reason and Other Works on the Theory of Ethics*. Translated by Thomas Kingsmill Abbott. 5th rev. ed. London: Longmans, Green, 1898.

———. *Religion within the Boundaries of Mere Reason*. Translated by Allen Wood. Cambridge: Cambridge University Press, 1998.

———. "Toward Perpetual Peace: A Philosophical Sketch." In *Toward Perpetual Peace and Other Writings on Politics, Peace, and History*. Edited by Pauline Kleingeld. Translated by David L. Colclasure. New Haven: Yale University Press, 2006. = "Zum ewigen Frieden." In *Kants Werke: Akademie Textausgabe*, vol. 8, *Abhandlungen nach 1781*. Berlin: de Gruyter, 1968.

———. *Toward Perpetual Peace and Other Writings on Politics, Peace, and History*. Edited by Pauline Kleingeld. Translated by David L. Colclasure. New Haven: Yale University Press, 2006.

Kelsey, David. *Eccentric Existence: A Theological Anthropology*. 2 vols. Louisville: Westminster John Knox, 2009.

Kemmerling, Andreas. "Was macht den Begriff der Person so besonders schwierig?" In *Gegenwart des lebendigen Christus*, edited by Günter Thomas and Andreas Schüle, 541–65. Leipzig: EVA, 2007. = "Why Is Personhood Conceptually Difficult?" In *The Depth of the Human Person: A Multidisciplinary Approach*, edited by Michael Welker, 15–44. Grand Rapids: Eerdmans, 2014.

Kessler, Wolfgang. "Wider die gefährliche Spaltung: Warum

Deutschland eine gerechtere Verteilung des Reichtums braucht." *Zeitzeichen* 20 (2000): 33.

Kirchhof, Paul. "Einführung in die Tagung." In *Die Menschenwürde als Verfassungsgrundlage, Essener Gespräche zum Thema Staat und Kirche*, vol. 51, edited by Burkhard Kämper and Klaus Pfeffer, 1–4. Münster: Aschendorf, 2019.

Kruse, Andreas. *Lebensphase hohes Alter: Verletzlichkeit und Reife*. Berlin: Springer Verlag, 2017.

Küng, Hans. *Global Responsibility: In Search of a New World Ethic*. Chestnut Ridge: Crossroad, 1991.

Lege, Joachim. "Die Herzkammer der Wissenschaft: Das Wissenschaftssystem braucht ein Zentrum, das bahnbrechende Erfindungen mit dem wissenschaftlichen und gesellschaftlichen Konsens vermittelt. Das können nur die Universitäten sein." *Frankfurter Allgemeine Zeitung*, September 19, 2019, N4.

Łuczewski, Michał. *Solidarity: Step by Step*. Warsaw: Centre for Thought of John Paul II, 2015.

Luhmann, Niklas. *Die Gesellschaft der Gesellschaft*. Frankfurt: Suhrkamp, 1997.

——. *Ökologische Kommunikation: Kann die moderne Gesellschaft sich auf ökologische Gefährdungen einstellen?* Opladen: Westdeutscher Verlag, 1986.

——. *Soziale Systeme: Grundriss einer allgemeinen Theorie*. Frankfurt: Suhrkamp, 1984.

——. "Soziologie der Moral." In *Theorietechnik und Moral*, edited by Niklas Luhmann and Stephan H. Pfürtner, 43–63. Frankfurt: Suhrkamp, 1978.

——. *Soziologie des Risikos*. Berlin: de Gruyter 1999.

Luhmann, Niklas, and Stephan H. Pfürtner, eds. *Theorietechnik und Moral*. Frankfurt: Suhrkamp, 1978.

Luther, Martin. *Werke, Kritische Gesamtausgabe*. Vol. 56. Weimar: Böhlau, 1938.

Marx, Karl. *Selected Writings*. Edited by Lawrence H. Simon. Indianapolis: Hackett, 1994.

Moltmann, Jürgen. *The Spirit of Life: A Universal Affirmation*. Minneapolis: Fortress, 1992.

―――. *Sun of Righteousness, Arise! God's Future for Humanity and the Earth*. Minneapolis: Fortress, 2010.

Müller-Armack, Alfred. *Wirtschaftslenkung und Marktwirtschaft*. Hamburg: Verlag für Wirtschaft und Sozialpolitik, 1947.

Naudé, Piet. *Pathways in Ethics: Justice—Interpretation—Discourse—Economics*. Stellenbosch: Sun Media, 2016.

Nida-Rümelin, Julian. *Demokratie und Wahrheit*. Munich: Beck, 2006.

Niebuhr, Reinhold. *Human Nature*. Vol. 1 of *The Nature and Destiny of Man*. New York: Scribner, 1964.

Nietzsche, Friedrich. *The Will to Power*. Translated by Walter Kaufmann and R. J. Hollingdale. Edited by Walter Kaufmann. New York: Vintage Books, 1968.

Nowak, Martin A. *Evolutionary Dynamics: Exploring the Equations of Life*. Cambridge, MA: Harvard University Press, 2006.

―――. "God and Evolution." In *The Science and Religion Dialogue: Past and Future*, edited by Michael Welker, 47–52. Frankfurt: Peter Lang, 2014.

―――. *Super Cooperators: Why We Need Each Other to Succeed*. New York: Free Press, 2011.

Nussbaum, Martha C. *Upheavals of Thought: The Intelligence of Emotions*. Cambridge: Cambridge University Press, 2001.

Pannenberg, Wolfhart. *Anthropology in Theological Perspective*. Edinburgh: T&T Clark; Philadelphia: Westminster, 1985.

―――. *Systematic Theology*. Translated by Geoffrey W. Bromiley. 3 vols. Grand Rapids: Eerdmans, 1994.

Parsons, Talcott. *The Social System*. New York: Free Press, 1951.

———. *Sociological Theory and Modern Society*. New York: Free Press, 1967.

Peters, Ted. "Entheokaric Freedom: Clarifying Confusions." In *Risiko und Vertrauen = Risk and Trust: Festschrift für Michael Welker zum 70. Geburtstag*, edited by Heike Springhart and Günter Thomas, 339–48. Leipzig: EVA, 2017.

Polkinghorne, John. "The Search for Truth." In *The Science and Religion Dialogue: Past and Future*, edited by Michael Welker, 53–59. Frankfurt: Lang, 2014.

Polkinghorne, John, ed. *The Work of Love: Creation as Kenosis*. Grand Rapids: Eerdmans; London: SPCK, 2001.

Polkinghorne, John, and Michael Welker. *Faith in the Living God: A Dialogue*. London: SPCK, 2001; 2nd ed., Eugene, OR: Cascade, 2019.

Pollack, Detlef, and Gergely Rosta. *Religion in der Moderne: Ein internationaler Vergleich*. Frankfurt/New York: Campus Verlag, 2015.

Pritchard, James B., ed. *Ancient Near Eastern Texts Relating to the Old Testament*. 3rd ed. Princeton: Princeton University Press, 1969.

Prodi, Paolo. *Eine Geschichte der Gerechtigkeit. Vom Recht Gottes zum modernen Rechtsstaat*. Munich: Beck, 2005.

Pröpper, Thomas. *Theologische Anthropologie*. 2 vols. Freiburg: Herder, 2011.

Ratzinger, Joseph. "What Keeps the World Together." In Jürgen Habermas and Joseph Ratzinger, *Dialectics of Secularization: On Reason and Religion*, edited by Florian Schuller, translated by Brian McNeil, 67–72. San Francisco: Ignatius, 2006.

Sauter, Gerhard. *Das verborgene Leben: Eine theologische Anthropologie*. Gütersloh: Gütersloher Verlag, 2011.

Schüssler Fiorenza, Elisabeth. "Slave Wo/men and Freedom in the Pauline Tradition: Some Methodological Reflections." In *Quests for Freedom: Biblical, Historical, Contemporary*, 2nd ed., edited by Michael Welker, 46–71. Eugene, OR: Wipf & Stock, 2019.

Schweiker, William. "Presenting Theological Humanism." In *Theological Ethics and Global Dynamics: In the Time of Many Worlds*, 199–219. Oxford: Blackwell, 2004.

Smit, Dirk J. "'Hope for Even the Most Wretched'? On Remembering the Reformation." *Stellenbosch Theological Journal* 4, no. 2 (2018): 703–25.

Soodalter, Ron. "A Blight on the Nation: Slavery in Today's America." In *Quests for Freedom: Biblical, Historical, Contemporary*, 2nd ed., edited by Michael Welker, 14–25. Eugene, OR: Wipf & Stock, 2019.

Soulen, R. Kendall, and Linda Woodhead, eds. *God and Human Dignity*. Grand Rapids: Eerdmans, 2006.

Springhart, Heike. *Aufbrüche zu neuen Ufern: Der Beitrag von Religion und Kirche für Demokratisierung und Reeducation im Westen Deutschlands nach 1945*. Leipzig: EVA, 2008.

Taupitz, Jochen. "Das hohe Gut der Wissenschaftsfreiheit: Forschung zwischen Erkenntnisgewinn und Risikoproblem." *Forschung und Lehre* 26 (2019): 446–47.

Taylor, Charles. *Hegel*. Cambridge: Cambridge University Press, 1975.

———. *Sources of the Self: The Making of the Modern Identity*. Cambridge: Cambridge University Press, 1989.

Theile, Gustav. "Das neue Jahrhundert der Religionen." *Frankfurter Allgemeine Zeitung*, October 27, 2019.

Theissen, Gerd. "*Sarx, Soma*, and the Transformative *Pneuma*: Personal Identity Endangered and Regained in Pauline Anthropology." In *The Depth of the Human*

Person: A Multidisciplinary Approach, edited by Michael Welker, 166–85. Grand Rapids: Eerdmans, 2014.

Thomas, Günter. *Gottes Lebendigkeit: Beiträge zur systematischen Theologie.* Leipzig: EVA, 2019.

———. *Implizite Religion: Theoriegeschichtliche und theoretische Untersuchungen zum Problem ihrer Identifikation.* Würzburg: Ergon, 2001.

———. "Vertrauen und Risiko in moralischen Hoffnungsgrossprojekten." In *Risiko und Vertrauen = Risk and Trust: Festschrift für Michael Welker zum 70. Geburtstag*, edited by Heike Springhart and Günter Thomas, 55–85. Leipzig: EVA, 2017.

Thomas, Günter, and Michael Welker. "Einleitung: Religiöse Funktionen des Fernsehens?" In *Religiöse Funktionen des Fernsehens? Medien-, kultur- und religionswissenschaftliche Perspektiven*, edited by Günter Thomas, 9–25. Opladen: Westdeutscher Verlag, 2000.

Thomas Aquinas. *Summa Theologiae.* Rochester: Aquinas Institute, 2012.

Tomasello, Michael. *The Cultural Origins of Human Cognition.* Cambridge, MA: Harvard University Press, 2001.

———. *Origins of Human Communication.* Cambridge, MA: MIT Press, 2008.

Tomasello, Michael, Malinda Carpenter, and Ulf Liszkowski. "A New Look at Infant Pointing." *Child Development* 78 (2007): 705–22.

Volf, Miroslav. *Flourishing: Why We Need Religion in a Globalized World.* New Haven: Yale University Press, 2016.

———. *Free of Charge: Giving and Forgiving in a Culture Stripped of Grace.* Grand Rapids: Zondervan, 2005.

Volf, Miroslav, and Justin Crisp, eds. *Joy and Human Flourishing: Essays on Theology, Culture and the Good Life.* Minneapolis: Fortress, 2015.

Weber, Max. *Economy and Society: An Outline of Interpretive Sociology*. Edited by Guenther Roth and Claus Wittich. Berkeley: University of California Press, 1978.

Weidinger, Nicole. *Gestik und ihre Funktion im Spracherwerb bei Kindern unter drei Jahren*. Wissenschaftliche Texte. Munich: Deutsches Jugendinstitut, 2011.

Weiler, Rudolf, ed. *Die Wiederkehr des Naturrechts und die Neuevangelisierung Europas*. Vienna: Verlag für Geschichte und Politik, Oldenbourg Verlag, 2005.

Welker, Michael. *Creation and Reality*. Minneapolis: Fortress, 1999.

———. "Die Anthropologie des Paulus als interdisziplinäre Kontakttheorie." In *Jahrbuch der Heidelberger Akademie der Wissenschaften für 2009*, edited by Heidelberg Akademie der Wissenschaften, 98–108. Heidelberg: Universitätsverlag, Winter 2010. = "Flesh—Body—Heart—Soul—Spirit: Paul's Anthropology as an Interdisciplinary Bridge-Theory." In *The Depth of the Human Person*, edited by Michael Welker, 45–57. Grand Rapids: Eerdmans, 2014.

———. "Flesh—Body—Heart—Soul—Spirit: Paul's Anthropology as an Interdisciplinary Bridge-Theory." In *The Depth of the Human Person*, edited by Michael Welker, 45–57. Grand Rapids: Eerdmans, 2014.

———. "God's Justice and Righteousness." In *Responsibility and the Enhancement of Life: Essays in Honor of William Schweiker*, edited by Günter Thomas and Heike Springhart, 179–90. Leipzig: EVA, 2017.

———. *God the Revealed: Christology*. Translated by Douglas Stott. Grand Rapids: Eerdmans, 2013.

———. *God the Spirit*. Philadelphia: Fortress, 1994. Reprint, Eugene, OR: Wipf & Stock, 2013.

———. "Habermas and Ratzinger on the Future of Religion." *Scottish Journal of Theology* 63, no. 4 (2010): 456–73.

―――. "Hans Küngs 'Projekt Weltethos': Gutgemeint—aber ein Fehlschlag." *Evangelische Kommentare* 26 (1993): 354–56.

―――. "Holy Spirit and Human Freedom: A John Paul II Memorial Lecture." *International Journal of Orthodox Theology* 8, no. 1 (2017): 9–30. Polish: "Duch święty i ludzka wolność." *John Paul II Memorial Lectures*, 181–96. Warsaw: Centrum Myśli Jana Pawła II / Konrad Adenauer Stiftung, 2018.

―――. "Introduction," 1–12. In *The Depth of the Human Person*, edited by Michael Welker, 45–57. Grand Rapids: Eerdmans, 2014.

―――. "Justice—Mercy—Worship: The 'Weighty Matters' of the Biblical Law." In *Concepts of Law in the Sciences, Legal Studies, and Theology*, edited by Michael Welker and Gregor Etzelmüller, 205–24. Tübingen: Mohr Siebeck, 2013.

―――. *Kirche im Pluralismus.* 2nd ed. Gütersloh: Kaiser Verlag, 2000.

―――. "The Power of Mercy in Biblical Law." *Journal of Law and Religion* 29, no. 2 (2014): 225–35.

―――. "Relation: Human and Divine." In *The Trinity and an Entangled World: Relationality in Physical Science and Theology*, edited by J. Polkinghorne, 157–67. Grand Rapids: Eerdmans, 2010.

―――. "Romantic Love, Covenantal Love, Kenotic Love." In *The Work of Love: Creation as Kenosis*, edited by J. Polkinghorne, 127–36. Grand Rapids: Eerdmans; London: SPCK, 2001.

―――. "Security of Expectations: Reformulating the Theology of Law and Gospel." *Journal of Religion* 66 (1986): 237–60.

―――. "The Spirit in Philosophical, Theological, and Interdisciplinary Perspectives." In *The Work of the Spirit:*

Pneumatology and Pentecostalism, edited by Michael Welker, 221–32. Grand Rapids: Eerdmans, 2006.

———. *Theologische Profile: Schleiermacher, Barth, Bonhoeffer, Moltmann*. Edition Chrismon. Frankfurt: Hansisches Druck- und Verlagshaus, 2009.

———. "Was ist Pluralismus?" In *Wertepluralismus*, Studium Generale der Universität Heidelberg 1998/99, edited by Christopher Balme, 9–23. Heidelberg: C. Winter, 1999.

Welker, Michael, ed. *The Depth of the Human Person: A Multidisciplinary Approach*. Grand Rapids: Eerdmans, 2014.

Welker, Michael, ed. *Quests for Freedom: Biblical, Historical, Contemporary*. 2nd ed. Eugene, OR: Wipf & Stock, 2019.

Welker, Michael, and Gregor Etzelmüller, eds. *Concepts of Law in the Sciences, Legal Studies, and Theology*. Tübingen: Mohr Siebeck, 2013.

Welker, Michael, and William Schweiker, eds. *Images of the Divine and Cultural Orientations: Jewish, Christian, and Islamic Voices*. Leipzig: EVA, 2015.

Whitehead, Alfred North. *Adventures of Ideas*. New York: Free Press, 1967.

———. *Process and Reality: An Essay in Cosmology*. Gifford Lectures 1927–28. Corrected ed. New York: Free Press, 1978.

———. *Science and the Modern World*. Cambridge: Cambridge University Press, 1953. Paperback ed., 2011.

Witte, John, Jr. *Church, State, and Family: Reconciling Traditional Teachings and Modern Liberties*. Cambridge: Cambridge University Press, 2019.

———. "Introduction." In *Christianity and Human Rights: An Introduction*, edited by John Witte Jr. and Frank S. Alexander, 8–43. Cambridge: Cambridge University Press, 2010.

———. "Law, Religion, and Metaphors." In *Risiko und Vertrauen = Risk and Trust: Festschrift für Michael Welker zum 70. Geburtstag,* edited by Heike Springhart and Günter Thomas, 177–94. Leipzig: EVA, 2017.

Wittgenstein, Ludwig. *Über Gewissheit, Werkausgabe.* Vol. 8. Frankfurt: Suhrkamp, 1984.

Zukowski, Tomasz, ed. *Values of Poles and the Heritage of John Paul II: A Social Research Study.* Warsaw: Centre for Thought of John Paul II, 2009.

INDEX